"The Wise Men and Women Have Sent Me to Tell You"

By Brother Marcus

Dedication Page:

"This book is wholeheartedly dedicated to Almighty God, my Creator and Saviour. I was hit by a drunk driver on April 22, 2005, and you graciously extended my life to continue working and serving your people. Thank you for another chance to get it right."

**Photos from the various youth events and workshops that
Marcus Girard has participated in
<u>over the last ten years:</u>**

Grateful Acknowledgements:

To my parents, to my immediate and extended family, to all the wonderful men and women, fathers, mothers, brothers and sisters, to all the members of my Nation and all of those whom I have had the pleasure of meeting, knowing, sharing and being in contact with in my life; Please accept this book as a small first offering from me as a testimony of the great knowledge, wisdom and understanding that you generously poured into my head from your exquisite souls and hearts. Thank you for every thing you have said to me and done for me that caused me to grow and to mature into a man. I pray daily that I will never forget what you did to help me along this journey that I am currently on. Thank you for helping me to become the man that I am becoming. Whatever and whenever I do, wherever and however I go, I will carry you in my heart, my mind and my spirit. You are indeed the Wise Men and Women who have sent me to tell them. I love you all...

Photos from the various youth events and workshops that Marcus Girard has participated in over the last ten years:

About the Author, Marcus Girard

Brother Marcus was born on November 15, 1972 to Joseph and Carol Girard. Marcus comes from a large family where he is the middle child of three older brothers and three younger sisters. Marcus is married to Cecelia Girard and they have six wonderful children together.

As a youth, Marcus grew up in a high risk, hard core inner city environment in Brooklyn, New York. Marcus lost many of his friends to drugs, gangs, guns and violence. As a youngster, Marcus was determined that one day, he would find a way to help people overcome the negative circumstances and difficulty factors that are a natural part of everyone's lives.

Marcus attended College at the esteemed and prestigious Morehouse College. In 1994, Marcus developed a company called the Youth and Adult Intervention Services. This company now has over fifteen years experience with both Youth and Adult Leadership Development and Motivational Self—Esteem Training. Marcus has personally worked with many diverse groups of youth that has ranged from the extremely at – risk to the most elite students in America. His presentations provide valuable insight into the current mindset of today's youth and adults.

Marcus has also developed several curriculums and programs that include Statewide Manhood and Fatherhood Training Program and workshops on topics such as Marriage and Family Relationships and Parent Empowerment. He has coordinated the Southwest Georgia Teen Fatherhood Program and worked with Teen Mothers in school systems. He has recorded several motivational CD's and is the author of the recently published book for males, **"The Wise Men and Women Have Sent Me to tell You."** Marcus also serves as the host of the extremely popular Internet Radio Talk Show, **"The Brother Marcus Show"**.

Marcus Girard is a natural communicator who has personally motivated tens of thousands of youth and adults. He is frequently called in by various organizations and churches to conduct leadership development seminars, parenting classes, and to motivate employees. Marcus Girard is a cultivator of the human spirit. His enlightening and illuminating presentations reach deep into the hearts and minds of audiences all over America and inspires self—improvement.

The Finest Motivational Speaking and Training to Youth and Adults in America!

Table of Contents

Chapter 1 – What is your life going to be about?

Hello and welcome to a special motivational book from the Brother Marcus Youth and Adult Intervention Services and Training Institute, Inc©®. This book is designed to share with you some very powerful guiding principles that will help you over the next few years into responsible manhood and leadership in your community. I have asked our Creator to guide my hands, my heart and mind as I wrote this book. I have read hundreds of motivational books and have listened to numerous motivational tapes in my lifetime. To me, it is totally insane for me to even attempt to motivate you without acknowledgment and consultation of your Creator. I believe this is one of the most rational and important things that anybody who works with people can ever do – consult the Creator for the best way that you may be of service to another person. I have learned the hard way in this work I am attempting to do of trying to uplift, to motivate, to inspire and guide human beings that I may have the right message but I may not be your particular Messenger. This principle is especially important as I work with children and young people.

I am a man who passionately loves and respects young people and I am also particularly concerned about our young men who are growing up in this day and time. I have had both the privilege and honor of working with tens of thousands of young men in the past fifteen years of my life. If the wise men and women had not guided me I would have very little to say to you. The valuable information in this book has been researched and pulled together for you from ideas from wise men and women from all over the world. This information was accumulated and adopted from many different sources. I believe if you will accept these ideas and principles into your personal life and philosophy, you will be more successful and happier in the coming days, weeks, months and years of your life. I truly commend you for being the kind of young man who understands the importance of striving to learn that little something extra that will give you certain advantages over the rest of your peer group.

Before we get started, I would like to thank Almighty God that He permits me to travel safety all over America and that He has blessed me with the skills and the resources to come to you in this way. I want to thank you for allowing me the privilege of sharing these life changing ideas and principles with you as you read this book. It is truly an honor for me to share any kind of message with young men, their parents or adults in general and I truly want to thank you in advance for taking the time to read this entire book. I have tried to make it entertaining and funny, yet educational at the same time. I recognize that you don't like to listen to some boring speaker or read boring material. Today, many young men believe like the rapper Eminem stated on the hook of one of his hit rap songs, **"Forgot about Dre"**:

"…Now-a-days everybody wants to talk like they got something to say. But nothing comes out when they move their lips, just a bunch of gibberish…"

Unfortunately, too many young men equate everything that most adults have to share with them to gibberish. I find that strange because many of our young men can't hold an intelligent conversation with adult men and women. Yet young men feel like it is adults who are wasting their time. Very interesting.

It is true that some people who don't know anything always want to tell you about it. It is very easy to think that we as adults are speaking gibberish to you. **I can promise you that what I have to say to you from the wise men and women may be forecasting your future if you don't listen to what we have to say.** The greatest realization I had in my life was the day when I realized that I didn't know enough to fit on the head of a very small safety pin. That's why I started listening to the wise men and women. My young brother, it's a great day in your life when you learn that you don't know everything nor can you know everything. When you compare all that you know to all that there is to know and learn in this world then you might feel the same way I did. *How much do you really know young brother?* While some of us as adults don't have much to say to you, I don't believe that you should dismiss *all of us* as irrelevant to your life. There are many adults who have a great deal of good to offer to young men. I have met many young men who don't know who their friends are and they don't know who their enemies are. *Is this true of you? Do you know who really has your best interests in mind as a young brother?* Maybe by the time you finish reading this book you will accept me as a friend or the big brother you have needed in your life. I am just your brother, Marcus. I did not drop down out of heaven but in fact I grew up in a little city up in the North called, Brooklyn, New York. Too many adults try to come at you and talk as if they are perfect and have never made any mistakes before. I can tell you with honesty, I have made plenty. I have had to live with the mistakes that I have made and that's one of the reasons I wrote this book for young men. I believe that if I can give you more knowledge, more wisdom and more understanding about life in general then you may be able to avoid the mistakes that I have made.

I want you to know that although we may have never met in person, I already have an abundance of love, honor and respect for youth everywhere. I believe the wise men and women have taught me correctly who you are and how great your future will be. With all the troubles that our young men constantly find themselves in these days, I still believe that your generation is the greatest generation that has ever lived. I really love your generation because I firmly believe that your generation is the one we have been waiting on for several millenniums. I want you to ask yourself these questions: *Of all of the times that you could have been born in the annals of human history, why are you alive in this day and in this time? Why are you alive to witness not just a brand new minute, or hour, or day, or week, or month, or year, or decade, or century, but why are you alive to witness a brand new millennium come in?*

The wise men and women have taught me that your generation does not represent hope. *You have been blessed to be born into a generation that represents fulfillment.* A couple can hope for a child for ten years. They can envision what the child will look like. Then one day a husband will join with his wife and then she will become pregnant. When that child emerges forth from the womb of its mother it may not look anything like either parent wanted, envisioned or desired. Well that's how your generation looks to many of the adults and the elders in our community. To many of them, your generation looks totally crazy! I mean think about it from the perspective of these adults for a minute. **Your generation talks, walks, acts, dresses, sings, mingles, dances, fights, parties and plays differently than every other generation that was here previously.** Your generation is often believed to not have any respect whatsoever for the elders and those who came before you. Unfortunately many young men believe that the elders should give respect to the young people before the young people should give respect to the elders. If that is true, then that is truly sad. If you disconnect from the people who preceded you onto the planet then you will be lost indeed. I believe that you should always strive to listen to the elder's wise council. That's why they have sent me to bridge the gap between the elders and the youth. The elders definitely need you, the strong, courageous young men but you also need them, the wise and the esteemed elders. The Scripture says it like this, **"Old men for council, young men for war."** If you don't listen to the wisdom of the elders then although you have the potential to be great, *you may never fully realize your potential.*

I have the blessing of working with young men everyday. Sometimes I just sit back and watch young men interact with each other. **Most young men make the critical mistake of thinking that their thoughts and their feelings are the only way to look at something or at someone.** Once some young men have thought on someone or something and made their conclusions then they naturally assume that their position is the right position. The wise men and women have said that the most powerful thing in the world is a made up mind. What have you already made up your mind about? One of my greatest frustrations with your generation is that I meet so many young men who have already made up their minds about the kind of life they are going to have before they ever really got started living.

I hate it that so many young brothers just want to play football, basketball or baseball for a living. I know that the Creator of my life and your life did not allow us to be born onto His planet to just catch some pigskin ball or to dunk some basketball. I mean that's wonderful to be able to do that and I'm not putting that down in the least. But there is so much that a young man can do and become in the world. You don't have to place all of your eggs in just those baskets. There is more to us than that. I have also met so many young men who only desire to be rappers. That's nice but what are you going to rap about? Will your rap be about more of the same kind of negative rap messages that is already out here on the airwaves? Are you going to tell us how it was growing up in the hood too? **Most of the rappers may have come from the hood but they don't live there anymore!** Young men have to expand their minds in terms of who they can be. You should allow no one to assign you a permanent place anywhere. I don't care where you were born in the world, you don't have to stay there all of your life.

One of the most important things for you to master is where you place your attention as a young man. I'd like for you to think ten years down the road as you read this book. **The wise men and women have sent me to tell you that if you learn to master your concentration you will be able to master anything.** You have got to learn how much you really do matter to your family, your friends, and to your school. And if you feel like you don't matter to them then think about your bigger family, your overall community and city. I like the hook to one of the rap songs that says, *"I put on for my city."* Notice that it's just the hook and not necessarily the some of the messages that the song promotes.

You will never have a bigger enemy in this world than your own self. Read that line over and over. After 35 years on the planet I have been able to successfully identify my biggest problem, ME! The same is true for you. The wise men and women told me that if you kicked the one who causes you most of your troubles, you would not be able to sit down for six weeks. You have known that all along and you knew it deep down inside... you just didn't want to admit it. But you are the problem and you have to get your own foot out of your own way. The way you do this is through the acquisition of more knowledge. We are never defeated unless we defeat ourselves. We defeat ourselves when we remain unknowledgeable.

One subject that I wish that young men would take more seriously in school is history. History is a wonderful subject for a young man to study. Some young men are failing the subject of history because we don't know its importance to our lives. **Of all our studies, history is the most attractive and is best qualified to reward the researcher. History is a young mans guide, for if he knows what was, then he will have a better understanding of what is. Then he will be more prepared for what is yet to come.** Just the other day you were a 'little bitty baby' in the womb of your mother. And when you were in the womb of your mother, you were a part of her history. And you were connected to her through what is known as an umbilical cord. It was only when you came out from the womb of your mother and the umbilical cord was cut, did time start for yourself and you began making your own history.

My teacher shared that right now you are history. What do I mean you are history? How are you history? How are you the past? Well, in you, is the genetic structure of your mother and your father or your genetic make-up. Many of you have seen pictures of your mother and father when they were younger and you probably look like them or some other relative in the family. Your genes are coded all the way back through your ancestry. Every prayer your ancestors ever prayed, every hope they ever hoped, and every dream they ever dreamed has been passed along from one relative to the next, down the line from the past to you here in the present. Now here you are in the present. Think over that for a moment. You are here and you are alive! What a blessing! Right now as a young man, you have a sperm in you that is for the future. As long as you are able to produce children into the world you have a future. But make no mistake about it; **your future depends on how well you do here with your life in the present.** I'll talk about that a little more later on in this book. But for now you have to accept that you are the past, the present and the future. Now why can't you master history? Knowing this should make the subject of history a lot more interesting to you because you are history. In fact, when you begin to really take a look at it you begin to understand that you are also mathematics. You come from a magnificent, mathematically precise Creator. He created your life to function on a mathematical level. How many times does your heart beat every minute? How much time does it take for blood to travel from the top of your head down to your toes and back to the top of your head again? What percentage of oxygen must you take into your body in order to breathe properly? Have you taken a study of each of the 206 bones of the human body that provide a framework for support of the body's soft tissues and organs while also being essential for movement? The reason you may not like school is probably because you never studied yourself. The reason you may not like school is because you see school as something that is separate and apart from you. But if you could only understand that you are Science, you are Art, and you are English and any and every subject that they could ever attempt to teach you at your school! **There is no subject that they can teach you in school that is not connected to you in some shape, form or fashion.** Young men need this understanding in order to become the masters of school and the masters of their education again.

As you are getting older there are a few things you will need to go out here and purchase to help you as you get started on your journey to manhood. One thing you will definitely need is a watch. You should always be able to know the time and what must be done. Your watch shouldn't be too gaudy but should help you by performing its most basic function, which is to help you tell the time. You should recognize that we are in some very dangerous times on this planet. **The wise men and women have sent me to tell you that what you will see over the next few years happening in the world is going to blow your mind.** You should always keep a pen and a pad present with you at all times. You never know when an emergency will strike when you will need to record some kind of useful information for yourself or for someone else. You will need a cell phone and two cell phone chargers. Cell Phones are most helpful and you must develop the discipline to keep yours active and working. So many young men already have cell phones but their cell phone is not making them any *legal* money. What a shame! Put your cell phone to work so that every time it rings it's a business call that you could make some legal money from versus a personal call with someone burning up your precious minutes. You will need at least two suits – preferably one blue and one black. You will need at least five white shirts that were fitted to your neck. You will need five to ten necktie combinations as well. You will need to learn how to tie a necktie properly. You will need several decent pairs of shoes as well to match your suit combinations. Learn how to shine your own shoes in a professional manner. You will need at least 10 pairs of dress socks for your shoes. You will need at least two pairs of sneakers for the days when you are casual. You will need at least 10 pairs of socks for your sneakers. You will need at least two jogging outfits. You will need at least 10 pairs of underclothes sets. You will need business cards that should include your name, an address and all of your telephone numbers you can be reached at. You will need a wallet. This wallet should contain your identification, your social security card and other important items. Do not leave home without it! Have a place at night where you place all of the stuff that you use on a regular basis. Keep your keys, wallet, umbrella, and cell phone all together in one place. **How many times have you spent hours looking for stuff that would have only required you to take a moment to find if you were better organized?** Learn to plan one day ahead of yourself. Then learn to plan a week out. Then learn to plan a month out. Then learn to plan six months out. Then learn how to plan one year out. Organization is the key to your life.

Let's go back to the human body again. The wise men and women have said that your body is a masterful organization of living tissue. You have many different organs operating in nine different systems. But this body is highly organized and, therefore, highly effective. It can adapt to every condition: extreme heat, extreme cold, high altitude, and below sea level. It will adapt. The human machine is highly organized.

The ant is highly organized also. No wonder Solomon said in the Bible, **"Oh, thou sluggard, study the ways of the ant and become wise."** Every civilization that has recorded its history records the presence of ants. The reason ants are not extinct is because they are highly organized. **Get organized young brother!** You will need to purchase a real camera. You will need film and batteries for the camera. You will need some pictures of yourself and your friends. Take lots of pictures of your mother, father, stepparents, and other family members. Take them today for you never know what tomorrow will hold for them or you. Everywhere you go take pictures. Every program that you participate in, take pictures. Everything that you do, take pictures. Purchase photo albums and scrapbooks and store your pictures in them. I have included a number of photos of the various workshops that I have conducted in this book for you to see. You will also need a planner and lots of pens. Always keep this with you. If you want people to take you seriously you have to have the appropriate materials. Get a drivers license as soon as you are able. Learn to drive. Learn to drive properly. Don't drive drunk. Don't speed. Know where you're going when you get into the vehicle. Do not have more than one person in the car with you as a young man if you can help it. Have no weapons or drugs of any kind with you. Once you know that you don't have any weapons or drugs on you then you have to make sure to keep company in your car that respect what you are about. If someone looks like they will place your life in danger because they just don't have good sense then don't let them ride with you. Make sure the car is clean, especially the trunk. If you are ever stopped by the police, respect their authority and do not be nervous at all. Be calm and respectful and slowly reach to give them whatever they may request of you.

Chapter Two – On the road to manhood

One of the main purposes of this book is to extend to you the knowledge that is yours by birthright. I have tried to include information in this book that a father figure, an uncle or an older brother should have taught you. By now, somebody should have told you that you were really a great young prince who was destined to be a world ruler. This book is your opportunity to read some of the same information that I share with young men all over America and refer back to when your life gets a little  discouraging. You have to learn how to take advantage of your own life force and develop your will to overcome obstacles in your pathway. If you don't desire to face the difficulties of life then you'll be just another young man walking around looking for someone to do for you what you could have gotten up and done for yourself. I cannot overemphasize why it is so important that you really begin to take a look at your life. Whether you are aware of this point or not, this is your moment in time. No one knows how long he or she has on this planet. As a young man it is so easy for you to become caught up. The life that you are shown every minute of every day on television, videos and movies may seem like it's calling your name. The street life may be calling your name. I am not sure what you are listening to that balances out what the rappers and hip-hop culture are offering you in terms of your personal values and morals. **We often don't realize how much today's music influences our values and what we hold as important in our lives.** Many young men attempt to argue that they are not affected in the least by the music that they listen to. They say only weak people are affected by what they listen to. **Hmmm....** Let me ask you a couple of questions: If you are not affected then why do you talk like you talk and spit the kind of game that you slang? If you are not affected then why do you think like you think? If you are not affected then why do you act like you act? Why do you dance as you dance? Why do you dress in certain kinds of clothes? Who made them hot? Why do you have an earring in your ear? Who made those sneakers or shoes the choice of your generation? What kinds of things interest you and why have those things captured your attention? What kinds of things are you involved in and why are you involved in those kinds of things? If we watch what you are doing then we can start to put a picture together about whom you are. If you are not concerned with you then how will you ever grow to be concerned with me or anybody else? Most young men may not understand that you are the microcosm of the macrocosm. What this means is that whatever is in the earth, a little bit of it is in you. So to understand great things in life you have to first try to understand the little things. That's why you are important. It is a fact that many young men don't think much of themselves. If your thinking doesn't change then you will continue to grow into a young man that doesn't think much of yourself or the family, or the community that produced you.

When you are about to take an action you should ask yourself, **"How will my actions affect my family and my loved ones?"** The challenge for you as a young man today is to think before you do things and not afterwards when you get into trouble. So many young men have done their first serious thinking about their life after they got into trouble with the law and had to do a little time in a Juvenile Detention Center or in some cases *"big boy"* jail. I don't know any mothers, who are happy to see their sons being sentenced to three, or six months or years in prison. Young men are committing such horrendous crimes that nowadays the courts and the judges are quick to send a young man to adult jail. I've watched many mothers heads drop in shame when the judge passed lengthy sentences down on their sons and even nowadays on their daughters. *So many young men claim to love their mothers and would do anything for their mothers but won't challenge themselves to do the right thing.* Your mother didn't bring you into the world 15 to 20 years ago to be standing in front of some judge. The doctors didn't smack you on your behind and say, **"This is a real pimp by blood not relation".** The doctor didn't say **"This is a true playa for real"** or **"This here is a true blood, or a real crip or a folk or a vice-lord"** when you were born. And the doctor also didn't say, **"Holla at a playa"** when you were born. Your Creator is not a gangbanger! While some of you are out here today trippin over your little block or your little silly set, your Creator is maintaining and managing an entire universe! Think over that for a moment. You are not a dog! You are not a pimp! You are not a playa! You are a young prince on your way to becoming a king. But you can't rule any kind of kingdom without more knowledge in your king dome (head)! Your problem is you listen to some of this crazy rap music and allow that to tell you who you are, where you are going, how you are going to get there, and who is going to help you. As a young man you are bombarded with ignorant thinking and utterances 24 hours a day on the radio and through these videos! Many of the negative rappers are quick to tell you about the fabulous lifestyle that they are leading. They never seem to get around to the consequences part of what will befall you if you partake in or become a party to the things that they are advocating for you to do in order to come up. There are consequences for the deeds that you do. You do indeed become guilty by association. You had better learn to think before you do and not afterwards. You need to keep people around you who are smarter than you who can challenge you to be a great somebody in life. A young man that is on his way to being a nobody in life is a dude that's out here doing nothing with his life and trying to mess up somebody else's life. There are plenty of these types of young men out here in the streets. You probably have a few around you on a daily basis.

A young man has to always be able to answer four important questions in his life at all times. Those questions are:

Who Am I?

Where Am I going?

How am I going to get there?

Who will help me to get there?

Your understanding of this will prove critical in the next ten years of your life. Remember, you will not always be 18, or 19, or 20 years old. You soon will be 28, 29 and 30. The most successful young man in ten years time will not be the cutest, the finest or the most handsome of you. The most successful will not be the one who lets his chain hang low till it wobbled to the floor or the one who robbed the jewelry store and told them to make him a grill. The most successful young man will not necessarily be the smartest or the most intelligent of you either. **You may find that the most successful young men in the next ten years will be those young men who were willing to do what the unsuccessful young men were unwilling to do.** You see a lazy young man will always estimate another young mans success as just pure luck. What most unsuccessful young men are unwilling to do is stop, take a look at themselves now and make the necessary changes that can improve their lives. Every young man reading this book can apply this principle in their lives and become a successful young man.

There's a rap song that was on the radio a few years ago by a group called 'Boyz N Da Hood". Let's look at the hook of one of their songs,

---

1. "Its some Boyz N Da Hood sell anything for profit (profit)
2. Five in the morning on the corner clockin' (clockin')
3. Yeah we wrong but dare a nig-- try to stop us (try to stop us)
4. And you can get it, anywhere anybody
5. Dem Boyz got work, Dem Boyz got yay
6. Dem Boyz got purp, Dem Boyz got haze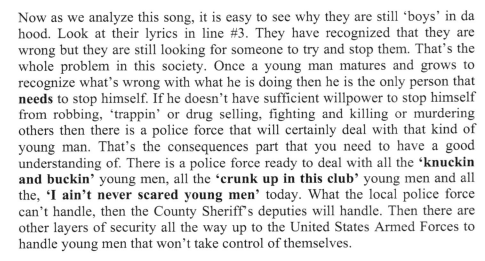
7. Dem Boyz got glocks, Dem Boyz got K's
8. Dem Boyz got blocks, Dem Boyz gettin paid

Now as we analyze this song, it is easy to see why they are still 'boys' in da hood. Look at their lyrics in line #3. They have recognized that they are wrong but they are still looking for someone to try and stop them. That's the whole problem in this society. Once a young man matures and grows to recognize what's wrong with what he is doing then he is the only person that **needs** to stop himself. If he doesn't have sufficient willpower to stop himself from robbing, 'trappin' or drug selling, fighting and killing or murdering others then there is a police force that will certainly deal with that kind of young man. That's the consequences part that you need to have a good understanding of. There is a police force ready to deal with all the '**knuckin and buckin**' young men, all the '**crunk up in this club**' young men and all the, '**I ain't never scared young men**' today. What the local police force can't handle, then the County Sheriff's deputies will handle. Then there are other layers of security all the way up to the United States Armed Forces to handle young men that won't take control of themselves.

Are you wrong as a young man? You have been blessed with parents, step parents, legal guardians, teachers, preachers and other folks in your community to help point out things that you need to improve in your life or things you need to work on. It is unfortunate that many parents in today's times don't understand that young people don't believe in the saying, **"Do as I say and not as I do"**. Even if your parents or others haven't been the best examples, after a certain point in your development you are supposed to be able to identify things that you need to correct in your own life. *Successful young men become successful by doing what they don't want to do when they don't want to do it.* In the adult world we call this 'self – discipline.' This life principle takes the place of your parent's advice and wise counsel. You need self-discipline in your life. It is the discipline that you impose on yourself that will help you to be 'a somebody' in life. You can't go anywhere in life without discipline. How disciplined are you? *Discipline means your ability to do the things that you really don't want to do.* A large percentage of adults lack discipline. Just watch an adult when they have to stand in line too long for something. We are fine as long as everything is moving along the way we desire it. But don't let something start to go wrong. We will start 'trippin' real hard. It's not easy to wait when you're young; delayed gratification is not an easy lesson to learn. In fact, maybe it's an art. It certainly is a discipline. It's going to take self - discipline in order for you to come up out of savagery into civilization.

From the word discipline you get the word disciple. All master teachers have students or disciples. What is a disciple? **A disciple is one who is in the process of being disciplined or is disciplining himself according to the teachings and the ways of a Master.** Are you anyone's disciple? Do you need to be? Remember all the 'Chinese movies' you saw when you were coming up. There was always someone who desired to be taught by the master fighter in those movies. Can you recall the attitude of the student? Didn't he always bow his head to his master? Bowing your head to the master is a sign that you are bowing the knowledge, wisdom and skill that is in your head to the knowledge, wisdom and understanding that the master will impart into your head. You will never become a master until you submit to a master. **So the question really becomes then, whose disciple are you?** Are you up under a master teacher? What is your proof that they are a master? Have they made any masters? If you are truly this person's disciple then they should be able to rebuke you. To rebuke means to criticize you or to reprove you sharply. It means that they can reprimand you. That person can check you or repress you and your desires. Are you really that person's disciple? Can this person really rebuke you? Would you run from their rebuke? Would you run from someone trying to check your wishes or desires? The wise men and women have taught me that people rebuke us because they love us. Therefore, in their rebuke is correction because they want us to be better than we presently are. We can never be what we really desire to be without correction, rebuke and exhortation. **You cannot be taught or trained without correction and rebuke.** There is no student of any teacher of any discipline that is not corrected in order to grow into the perfection of that discipline. **The more correction one is given, the greater they are demonstrating their love for you.** If a person who claims to love you won't take the time to help you become more disciplined then that should make you a little suspicious. If you want to be a great servant of others then you must become a master of yourself.

Young men need correction so badly in their lives. Yes, young women need correction very bad as well. But this is a book for young men! You can't tell me that you don't need to have someone help you to discipline your morals. When you allow a wise master to come into your life then they will begin to help you to work on yourself. They will help you to spot your character defects. Once those defects are identified this person should help you to manipulate the defects and help you to deal with them effectively. **We all have character defects.** Defects are our imperfections that impair our worth or utility. A defect is a lack of something that is necessary for completeness, adequacy or perfection. A defect is a deficiency. Character defects include laziness, indolence, slothfulness, talking too much, being nosy, lying and cheating, and being envious and jealous. If an evil person finds out your character defects they can turn the power of your being against you. They can neutralize you because they are fighting you and using your own weaknesses against you.

Many young men fight against anyone having any measure of control over their lives. Anyone who emerges to discipline you is in for the fight of his or her life. I have worked with tens of thousands of young men and I am working to discipline four sons right now and it's like training wild animals. When the trainer first meets the animal it's wild and ferocious. The trainer has to whip the animal or lash it to get it to do what the trainer wants done. This process generally goes on in private where no one can see. The trainer does this to bend the will of the animal to do what he wants it to do. The trainer doesn't want to hurt the animal, but he has a job to do by the animal. His job is to prepare the lion, the elephant or that animal in such a way that when it comes in front of the public that animal will do exactly what it is supposed to do without fail! This is very similar to the process that you will have to go through. Somebody has to help you tame your wild passions and help you to get control of an out of control nature. **A master will help you to attain moral excellence and firmness of character because they are committed to the process of disciplining you.** They are not beating you with their hands, fists, cords, chains or whips. You don't need that kind of discipline from this person but that may have to come in your life if you don't learn to listen. **What do I mean?** Look again at the police officers in our community. They are armed to the teeth. They have a semi-automatic weapon or a glock, a bulletproof protective vest, and all the necessary belt gear. This may include a taser gun, a billy club or night stick, mace, pepper spray, and don't forget many of them have an assault rifle in the trunk of their cars. As a police officer goes about his / her duties, it is as though they are in a huge cage with violent beasts that they must protect themselves from as they try to establish some degree of order by means of enforcement of law. That's what is waiting for you if you don't get your act together.

The master that I want you to recognize may already be in your life. Right now this person should be giving you training that is correcting you, molding you, or perfecting your mental faculties and moral character. Again, who are you allowing to help you become disciplined? Have you learned how to discipline yourself? A young man can become wise by observing carefully what happens when he isn't wise. You should discipline yourself now so others won't have to later.

Since we are on this subject, did you know that the building of prisons is the number one growth industry in America? The prison industrial complex is so big that it is on the stock market. They're going to build more, and more, and more prisons. Why? Who are they building them for? People do not build hotels because they **do not** expect occupancy. Businessmen are investing in prisons that they *intend* to fill. In every major city in America, and even minor cities, who is filling up the funeral parlors? It is our young men ages 18 to 35, either killed by AIDS, gunshot wounds, drug overdoses or suicide. It costs nearly $40,000 a year to keep a man in jail. America now has over 2 million people in prisons and nearly 6 million people on probation or parole. **Did you know that it is estimated that 85% of all youths sitting in prisons grew up in fatherless homes?** In the black community single black females head 70% of all black households in America. What kind of home are you growing up in? Is there a man somewhere? Some of the penologists and those who are in charge of prisons are saying that today's youth are committing crimes of violence more heinous, colder and more callous than anything that they have ever seen in the past. Violence now has become the order of the day in America. In fact about it, America is the most violent crime ridden society on the earth. If you end up in prison today you could also end up becoming a human guinea pig that is experimented on regularly. You also run a very high risk of being raped and violated in prison as well. The prisons in America used to be known as penitentiaries. The goal was to make you penitent or sorry over what you had done to end up in prison in the first place. I have met many young men who went to the Youth Development Campus's and to Regional Youth Development Campus's. Very few if any were sorry over what they did. They did seem very sorry over the fact that they got caught. Remember this! Many male prisoners read at a third grade level. On their release from prison in most cases they won't be able to find even unskilled jobs. That is why almost two-thirds of former prisoners return right back to prison.

Everything is connected. Consider for a moment, what you spend the majority of your time doing? Are you able to share something that you have mastered? *Mastery is right in your own nature. The Creator has put that in you. Whatever you choose to make the center of attention for any long length of time you will eventually master.* That is the greatest secret in the world. You just need more patience with yourself as a young man. So many young men consider it too painful to be patient. You could be a great young man right now if you were not so worried about having fun, and what your boys were doing or worrying about some girl. So many young men are only striving to master the X-box or the Play Station. Some young men may already believe that mastery is for someone else to accomplish and that they personally will never accomplish anything of any real or lasting value. Many young men are quick to tell me about entertainers and sports figures whose talent they wouldn't mind having. They are quick to tell me about people out here with money that they wouldn't mind having. I ask them, **"Why do you think entertainer's, sport's figures and rich people are where they are and the majority of other people in the world are where they are?"** What is the real reason? I tell them, **"If you aren't doing anything with the talent, the money, or the skills that you currently have then what makes you think that you would do something with the talent, the money, or the skills that someone else has?"** Are you willing to practice your craft or develop your skills hour after hour, day after day, and year after year? That's how the entertainers do it. That's how the sport's figures do it. That's how they have developed their skill to the point that their manifestation of the skill is attractive to thousands of people. That's how they are able to make those big dollars that you lust after. **Most young men give very little time, often nothing, to do the things they say they would give anything to do.**

Do you come from a home environment where people are about the business of mastering things? You might say, **"Well no one in my current family or in the history of my family was or is a master of anything."** Many of us come from families who have only mastered negative things. Maybe you come from a family that has only mastered drinking liquor or mastered smoking weed and rolling blunts. The family that smokes together chokes together. Maybe some of the members of your family have mastered murdering and killing. I have met some young men who shared with me that all of the men in their family were locked up. That may be true and that is sad. **It is sad to come from a family where no one wants to even attempt the uphill road.** One of the greatest purposes of parents is to teach their children how to live successfully and zestfully. I believe that is one of the greatest responsibilities of parents and I also believe that is one of our greatest failures as parents today. It is pitiful what passes as family life today.

Even if you come from a good home, which many of you do, there are a host of issues that you must deal with on a daily basis like your basic survival. Did you know that **homicide is the primary cause of death for black males between the ages of thirteen and twenty-five?** The threat of violence to young black males comes from many sources: crime within the black community, mistaken identity, drug-related incidents, gang activity, police brutality, and a host of others. No amount of money, education, and celebrity status can guarantee the safety of a black man in America.

Some parents don't adequately prepare their families for the eventual reality that they won't be here one day. You are going to one day be confronted with everything your parents are dealing with right now. **You need to learn how to do everything for yourself.** The following is a brief list of things you should learn right now from somebody if you really just don't know or fully understand:

1. **You need to learn how to clean up after yourself.** Stop being a slob. You need to learn how to keep a house from top to bottom. Learn how to sweep and mop properly and you need to learn how to dust. You need to learn how to paint. You need to learn how to vacuum. You need to learn how to take your clothes off at the end of the day and put them in a hamper. The way you keep your room is a sign of the way you will keep your house.

2. **You need to learn or gain a general idea of how things work.** No one is asking you to take stuff apart and leave it like that but develop an interest in how things around you work. As you get older you will need at least a basic knowledge of tools, cars, plumbing, carpentry, computers, refrigeration, air conditioning, electricity and lighting, television and cable, and audio and visual. If you don't learn to do these things for yourself then you will always be a consumer of goods and services versus being a producer of the goods and services that you need. Every young man needs to learn how to work with his mind and his hands.

3. **You need to learn more about the outdoors.** You need to learn how to mow and how to rake. There is nothing wrong with learning a little gardening as well. You need to learn about where food comes from. You probably don't want to hear anything about farming yet farming is the engine of every nation. America would not be America today were it not for farmers. I thank God for the farmers and I tell you as a young man that you should learn something about farming. In the future you will need to provide for yourself the things that you consume. You may end up owning a farm and raising on your farm

the necessities of life. *In our communities, we need to be better examples to you as adults!* We build all these big, majestic, mega churches but we don't build any big, majestic, mega-supermarkets in the community. We need to buy some land and instead of building beautiful churches we need to build up some supermarkets. You've seen many supermarkets in your city but have you ever thought about building your own supermarket? You could have a supermarket in every city in America. You could open up canning factories and frozen food factories so you could take your products from the ground, can it or freeze it, and put it into our own supermarkets. **What's wrong with a church owning a canning factory?** What's wrong with the different churches producing the peas, the corn, the asparagus, and the carrots that we all eat? I wouldn't shop anywhere else except in our own supermarket. Before you know it, the money that we spend on food is right back in our circle, growing. In the past, you should have learned that we used to pick cotton. What's wrong with picking it again this time for our own direct benefit? We can turn the cotton into lint, and the lint into cloth. All of you reading this book hopefully have on underwear, yet in our community we haven't produced one pair of underwear. How are you going to make a rap songs talking about **'You are the biggest boss that we've seen thus far'** and you don't even produce the underwear that you put on? We don't produce toilet paper in our community. And you're a boss? **Please! You're a consumer.** As adults, we need to set up underwear factories to help our young men get employed. Now, instead of designer underwear from Calvin Klein, you can put your name on it. Then everybody in America is wearing your underwear! The underwear market can be yours, the shirt market can be yours, the suit market can be yours! The same way other folks can get the hide of an alligator and turn that into alligator shoes, we can get them too. The gator doesn't belong to them exclusively, God created it! The cow that gives his hide to people in other communities will give it to you too young man. You can learn the skills to tan that hide, and make you some shoes. It's a shame you're paying $150 to $190 for Nike shoes, and all we have to do is learn how to make our own brand of sneakers and buy it from ourselves. If we did that we would get a whole economic revolution started in our community. You have to think like this in order to take control of your own destiny as a young man.

4. **You should learn how to cook for yourself.** The wise men and women taught me that we dig our graves with our teeth. You need to learn how to eat to live and how to properly nourish your body. As a

young man you cannot be unwilling to learn the art and science of cooking. You have to spend time shopping and learn how to avoid buying chemically prepared foods that someone has already prepared in their kitchen that you have never seen. When we eat chemically prepared foods, it remains in your colon, hardening into a stone-like lump. You need to learn how to cook more than Ramen Noodles, which has a great deal of salt in each little package. You would be surprised at the high amounts of salt in most of the food today. Learn how to prepare whole meals for your family. Learn how to bake. Learn what to eat and what not to eat. The wise men and women have taught me that everything was not meant for human consumption. I personally do not recommend for you to try eating all the different types of foods that there is. Try and eat fresh foods and not stale foods. Cook it done, and not half done. By the way you should purchase a set of stainless steel cooking utensils to cook your food in.

5. **You need to learn how to shop.** You need to learn how to buy clothes that fit you. You need to learn how to shop for others. Your tastes may not necessarily be the tastes of your friends and loved ones. You need to learn how to shop inexpensively. You need to learn how to coordinate your colors. You also need to learn how to save some money. You should never spend every dime that you get.

6. **You need to learn how to sew.** You don't need to throw clothes away because a stitch has become undone. Sewing can make you rich and famous, if you're talented enough - just look at designers like P – Diddy, Jay Z and Russell Simmons.

7. **You need to learn how to study and research information.** You need to purchase a computer and gain access to the Internet. Every possible subject or topic that you would want to know more about is on the World Wide Web. You need to learn how to access the information you need on the Internet. You will need to purchase books on word etymology. You will need dictionaries and thesaurus's as you get out in the world and began to understand more things.

8. **You need to learn how to access the various automated telephone systems for information.** It can be very frustrating to speak with customer service representatives for your telephone, cell phone, light, gas, electricity or cable concerns. Most companies have instituted call centers to handle your calls. Estimated wait times are usually 25 – 40 minutes before someone picks up. This is by design. They don't want to really talk with you and that's why they make you wait and wait and wait. They hope that you will hang up the phone and give up. They just want your money. Understanding this from the very

beginning should aid you in developing the patience that you need in order to get what you need to get accomplished.

9. **You need to learn how to relax without the use of drugs and alcohol having to be present.** You need to learn how to handle stress. You need to learn how to handle disappointment and frustration properly. You will need to learn how to deal with people in general. So many young men are in complete disbelief when I share with them that I have never used or sold drugs or drank any alcohol in my life. Yes, it is true. Right now, with the tremendous stress that I am under, I have never even considered using crack, smoking weed, snorting some powder or popping some pills in order to cope with the realities of my life. Drugs and alcohol have not now nor ever been anything I'm interested in. By God's grace and mercy, He has kept me from that. I've seen the effects that using drugs and alcohol has had on many of my friends and the people that I grew up with and their bad example was good enough for me.

10. **You need to learn how to deal with females.** You will have to learn what it means to be committed to a female. I will discuss them a little further in this book.

11. **You will need to learn how to drive.** You must get a driver's license as soon as possible. Having transportation that you are legally able to drive is truly a great blessing and privilege to have.

12. **You will need to learn how to feel.** Are you your brothers' keeper? Do you feel his pain and his anguish? Is his hurt your hurt? Do you really love the brotherhood? Could your friends trust you with their girl or are you a flirt too? How will you learn to love for your brother what you love for yourself?

These are just a few of the things that you will have to learn in your life. That's why you must learn how to build an extended family. That's why you must learn to befriend other people, who are perhaps not blood relatives, but they can grow closer to you than your own brothers and sisters. I have developed friendships with thousands of people who are members of my extended family. It's relatively easy for me to make new friends. The wise men and women have said that there is something in every man and woman of mastery. I look for the mastery of skills in others. Even if I may not have that skill I get tremendous joy watching them exercise their mastery and skill. What you have to understand is that every man and woman is your superior in something. Be mindful to always be respectful of adults. Look for the best in us as adults. Once you have judged us as adults the wrong way you often feel like there is nothing we can tell you. Twenty years down the line I can promise you that you will end up suffering from the pain of discipline or the pain of regret. The wise men and women have told me that the pain of discipline will only weigh ounces compared to the pain of regret, which will weigh tons. There are so many adults out here today who live in the pain of regret. They are always talking about how they would of, they could have, and should have done but they didn't.

Boys in the hood who don't desire to impose self-discipline in their lives never grow up to be real men. They grow up to be false men who never experience what true manhood or power feels like. They mistakenly think their power comes from carrying and using guns, or selling some weed, crack or other illegal substance to addicted people all during the day and night. But how much strength does it take to further destroy a man that's already weak? One day we are going to get rid of drugs completely in America.

All of us already have things and people and circumstances and stuff in our lives that we need to deal with. The wise men and women sent me here to tell you that time, circumstances and events shape our thinking. Problems don't disappear; they grow bigger and stronger in our lives if we don't do anything about them. You have to know that the Creator of your life has equipped you with everything that you need to deal effectively with your problems. Everyone that is alive has got some problem to solve. Dead people are the only ones that have no problems. If you didn't want to deal with problems you should never have been born. Men actively work to grow in knowledge, wisdom and understanding too not only deal with their problems but to help others deal with theirs.

One of the main reasons that so many young men won't face their problems or their issues is because they lack character development. This is why they have movies called Boys in the Hood and not Men in the Hood. We will remain 'boyz' until a real man emerges to bring 'boyz' into true manhood. And that real man may already be present in your life. He might be your father. He might be your stepfather. He might be your Principal, Assistant Principal, Counselor, Teacher, Coach, Janitor or some other male in your life that is trying to model true Manhood to you. Many young men do not like the authority that a man yields. That's only because there is a budding man in you trying to emerge that's conflicting with the established man that's in front of you. You will never become a real man without a **REAL** man to bring you into manhood. Men have to help a boy come into manhood. Many young men have "punkish" ways and attitudes that they have adopted into their lives. Some young men manifest their feminine side more than their masculine side. Some young men mistakenly think that everyone is going to bow down and run because you have screwed up your face and don't like this or that. **Young men have to have someone who is fit and ready at every possible moment to challenge that lazy, jive, trifling, selfish, ugly - acting, procrastinating, antagonistic, trouble making, smart talking, disrespectful, rebellious part of you!** One of the main reasons that there is so much chaos in our community today among our youth is because there aren't enough real men around to do that for boys and girls in today's times. If you don't have anyone around your life that is willing to help you with that critical part of your life I recommend that you hurry and join some Male Leadership Development program to help you along.

Chapter Three - Who are you?

You should actively be trying to find out who you are as a young man. When I was younger I can remember asking a man at my High School, **"When will I know that I have become a man?"** That man looked at me firmly and said, *"When you understand the difference between the two things that I am about to tell you. Boys are always found doing what they want to do while men are always found doing what they have to do. When you understand the difference between what you want to do versus what you have to do then you will be on the road to becoming a man"*. I never forgot that profound statement. Boys do what they want to do while men do what they have to do. Young men with a childlike mentality and mindset are totally focused on what they want to do. They only think of what will be fun and pleasurable and make them feel good while a man is focused on his duties and responsibilities in life and what they have to do. They willingly choose to focus on the task at hand, no matter how big or how small. Surprisingly, it is after they complete the task that they started out to complete that they find their joy in life! *Let me ask you a question: Are you still doing what you want to do or have you begun the process of doing what you have to do as a young man?*

Would you say that the impressions that you have about your identity are true and valid? Are your impressions of yourself mostly negative or positive? Our negative and positive attitudes about ourselves started forming when we were little children. If you have developed a negative attitude or disposition from your childhood then you have some work to do to change that. As we get older if nothing drastically changes or alters a negative attitude then most of the time it hardens into a belief system. Just imagine if someone fed you false and negative ideas, false and negative concepts and false and negative information about who you really were since you was a little boy. Sometimes false ideas, false concepts and false information are passed on from one generation to another generation.

The effect of instant rejection has an immeasurable effect on a child. When a person thinks they are physically unpleasing to the eyes of others, they believe that everyone who meets them thinks they are ugly too. The attitudes that we perceive we get from other people, is what we expect. It amazes me to go into schools to talk to our young people. I generally ask them, **"How many of you believe you are beautiful or handsome?"** Sometimes not one hand goes up among the girls or the boys. It is a shame that so many adults have produced children and did not spend adequate time building them up from the inside to the outside. As you read this book, I would like for you to think about the seeds that were dropped on you when you were a little child that have now taken root.

Who are you? What interests do you have? Many of our young men don't seem to be interested in anything. Maybe that's why they are not very interesting. It's hard to hold an intelligent conversation with many young men because they don't have knowledge of much of anything. **One of the ways that a young man becomes interesting is by first becoming interested in different things.** In other words, stop twisting your hair and start to take notice of things that are happening around you. Another question for you to consider is what are your special talents? What are your expectations of the world and what is the world expecting from you? Does the world owe you something or do you owe the world something? You may not know this but the Creator of all of our lives has given every young man gifts and talents from Himself. It is your duty to get those gifts, talents and skills out of you into the world so that everyone will know who you are. A man is known by what he does. Just stating your name to someone means nothing. Who cares? Who cares who your parents are? The wise men and women taught me that you've got to do your own growing, no matter how tall your father was. How are you representing your parents to the world if you are about nothing? You can't live off of what they are doing right now or have already done. Every tub has to sit on its own bottom. Parents should strive to give you the best possible starting point but ultimately you have to go out into the world and make your name mean something as a young man. Many parents often name their children after famous men who have died. That doesn't mean anything at all to have the name of a great man if you aren't going to be about something. There are many men in jail right now as you read this with the name Martin Luther King. The only way you can begin to see what the Creator has placed within you is to begin the process of acquiring knowledge. You have to read books. You have to read the biographies and autobiographies of great men and women who have lived and died but they or someone else thought enough of you to write down an account of their life and times.

First, you have to want to read. Two of the lost arts that I now see among your generation are the arts of reading and writing. **What kind of young man doesn't like to read?** Most young men do not understand the importance that reading plays in their lives. Reading is the foundation of your life. The wise men and women have taught me that every year in American High Schools, 10% to 30% of the students graduate as 'functional illiterates.' What is a functional illiterate? A young man who is considered functionally illiterate is able to read and write in the English language. However, he does so with a very low degree of grammatical correctness, speed, and style, and cannot perform fundamental tasks such as: filling out an employment application; following written instructions; reading a newspaper article; reading traffic signs; consulting a dictionary; or understanding a bus schedule. In short, when confronted with printed materials, young men without basic literacy skills cannot function effectively in modern society. Functional illiteracy also severely limits interaction with information and communication technologies (i.e. using a personal computer to work with a word processor, a web browser, a spreadsheet application, or using a mobile phone) adequately or efficiently. Young men that are functionally illiterate may be subject to social intimidation, health risks, stress, low income, and other pitfalls associated with their inability.

The correlation between crime and functional illiteracy is well-known to criminologists and sociologists throughout the world. In the early 2000s, it was estimated that 60% of adults in federal and state prisons in the United States were functionally or marginally illiterate, and 85% of juvenile offenders had problems associated with reading, writing, and basic mathematics.

Now be honest with yourself. Are you becoming a functional illiterate in school right now? I once read a story about a donkey who carried a bag of books up a mountain on his back for four straight years. He eventually got to the top of the mountain but he still was a donkey. You may be wondering why? Because all he did was carry the books on his back! He never opened any of the books to read them! Do you get the point? Carrying books will never take the place of reading them. Some young men I know are just like that donkey in the story. They go to school everyday. They go to class all the time and carry their books in a bookbag on their backs. After four years they will probably even graduate from their schools. But they never study anything at home. They never do homework. They rely on their suaveness, their cuteness, their charm, their wit, their coolness, their hustle and flo to get by. Some of them are cheaters. Poor young man. They don't see tomorrow coming. The lessons that somebody is trying to teach you today will make a lot more sense tomorrow. Study the concept of school. The whole object of school is to teach you some lessons well enough that when the test or exam comes you can pass and go on to the next lesson. In life it is the same way. In school you may have teachers that you just don't like. The feeling may indeed be mutual. The teacher's job is to teach the subject in such a way that it compels you to want to learn more about it. The teacher's job is to attract your mind to the subject and make you see it's relevancy to your life now or in the future. If the teacher is a good teacher then their instruction and guidance in that subject helps to prepare you for the work you will be doing down the road. Life is the same way. Life is going to teach you some pretty deep lessons and concepts. You have to be a good student in life just like you have to be in school. The teachers that life chooses to teach you the lesson may not be your choice. The important thing is that you learn the lessons that life is trying to teach you. **Are you caught up in what the teacher is or is not or are you caught up in the lesson that they are there to teach you?**

I have had many teachers in my life and I still have many teachers in my life. You never reach a point in this life where you cannot be taught something by someone. As long as you are alive you will always have teachers and you will always be used to teach others. Remember this though. Some young men flunk certain classes because they don't like the teacher. Eventually they have to take the same class over even if it's with another teacher. Life is the same way. There are certain life lessons that are so important for you to learn and pass that until you learn them you will have to keep repeating them over and over. You must be tried and tested in school and you will be tried and tested in life.

Young man, you will always be a small time young man if you don't like reading and if you don't like writing. **I can promise you that your personal ignorance will always keep you on the bottom.** As long as you do not know how to read with understanding, you will always be looking at somebody else, blaming him or her for your condition; but it is not anybody's fault. You have to get up and read in order for you to evolve from one stage into another. Reading and writing are useful ways to convey ideas and information, which are essential in society today. It is only through reading that your intelligence is developed. When you open a book, it looks like a bird with open wings. When you learn to read with understanding, when you can open the book of knowledge, when you can understand what you read, then that is like giving yourself wings in which to fly. There is no condition that human beings suffer from in the world that cannot be overcome with knowledge.

Reading is crucial to being an informed citizen. You soon will have the right to vote when you turn 18. You may already be 18 or older. You can't be an informed voter if you haven't read what the issues are and know where the candidates stand on those issues. As you get older you will be given thousands of documents to sign. May I give you some hard learned advice? **You should sign nothing without reading it first.** Never keep people around you who don't read or like to read. Reading information will give you something to talk about. After three days without reading, our conversations often become flavorless. Remember that a person who can read but doesn't has no advantage over the person who can't read at all. You have to learn the English language in order to enjoy reading. You have to know how to speak the English language. I know that it is difficult to develop the discipline of reading and researching information. But if you don't read and analyze things for yourself then how can you trust that someone will share information with you properly? Make it a practice to read three newspapers a day. Make it a practice to watch the local, regional and national news every day. Make sure you get the latest magazines that have relevant information to tell you about how you can do more with your life. Your life is the main goal. Don't try to be anyone else, learn to love you. The more you can read and understand what you are reading, the more your personal happiness will increase. Reading books help you to build your mind. Reading will better acquaint you with some of life's greatest and worst moments in human history. If you cannot read get help. There are all kinds of agencies that are in your city to help you. Ask and you shall receive. He who is afraid of asking is ashamed of learning. ***He who asks a question is a fool for five minutes; he who does not ask a question remains a fool forever.*** One of the ways that you get knowledge is to open your mouth and ask. Asking is the beginning of receiving. Many young men unfortunately will remain behind in life because they are too proud to ask for help. Just think how many questions have gone unanswered in your life because you didn't want anyone to think that you didn't have the answer. How much worry has already eaten out your insides because you didn't want to ask for help? Asking is one of the hardest things you will ever do because it assumes a position of need. Why would the Scriptures ask us to ask? To ask is to depend on someone other than yourself. It is very humbling. You are not that cool as a young man that you don't have to occasionally ask questions. I am always asking questions. The National Enquirer Magazine used to have an ad that said, **"Enquiring minds want to know."** If you don't ask you will not receive anything. Don't just ask one person, ask everybody. I repeat, there are adults in your city that can help you right now. You should also practice writing. How is your handwriting? How is your penmanship? How well can you spell? You can't be this great big time person you are destined to be and can't spell, can you? Can you write clear and concise sentences? How can you be on the big time level that you are always talking about being on if you don't know the parts of speech which includes the proper use of verbs, nouns, pronouns, adjectives, adverbs, prepositions, conjunctions, and interjections?

Let me ask you a question. How are you talking about making big money one day and you don't like math? I'm not trying to put you down; I'm trying to pick you up. I'm asking twenty-one questions. **I wish that I had taken school more seriously.** I wish that I had paid more attention in my Sciences, History, Spanish and Math classes. Again, you are not always going to be 15 to 20 years old. One day you are going to be 25 and 35 and 45. I'm talking about the days when you may not be cool any more. I'm talking about the days when perhaps you will be married to your wife with three or four children around you. I'm talking about the days when there will be a whole new generation of young people with brand new styles and flavors. I know many young men who don't care two cents for school. All they know how to do is disrupt and act the fool. They know how to tear another young man down but they don't know the art or the science of how to build a young man up. One day I know they will be sorry. I know I was. Now I'm a grown man with children trying to learn the stuff I should have learned years ago. Don't let people tell you that you won't need that mess they are teaching you down at that school. That's wrong. You can always use knowledge in some shape, form or fashion. Try using ignorance. Ask the person who is telling you that you won't need it what they are doing with their life. Ask them to tell you what you will need. The wise men and women told me to tell you to get as much knowledge as you can to fit into the 14 billion brain cells that the Creator has put into your brain. *Consider these statistics:*

- Every 29 seconds another student gives up on school, resulting in more than one million American high school students who drop out every year
- Nearly one-third of all public high school students—and nearly one half of all African Americans, Hispanics and Native Americans—fail to graduate from public high school with their class
- There are nearly 2,000 high schools in the U.S. where 40 percent of the typical freshman class leaves school by its senior year
- The dropout problem is likely to increase substantially through 2020 unless significant improvements are made
- Dropouts are more likely than high school graduates to be unemployed, in poor health, living in poverty, on public assistance, and single parents with children who drop out of high school
- Dropouts earn $9,200 less per year than high school graduates and more than $1 million less over a lifetime than college graduates

- Dropouts were more than twice as likely as high school graduates to slip into poverty in a single year and three times more likely than college graduates to be unemployed in 2004
- Dropouts are more than eight times as likely to be in jail or prison as high school graduates
- Dropouts are four times less likely to volunteer than college graduates, twice less likely to vote or participate in community projects, and represent only 3 percent of actively engaged citizens in the U.S. today
- The government would reap $45 billion in extra tax revenues and reduced costs in public health, crime, and welfare payments if the number of high school dropouts among 20-year olds in the U.S. today, which numbers more than 700,000 individuals, were cut in half

As I researched the Drop Out Problem in America online I found that it was referred to as **America's Silent Epidemic.** If you are a young man that has dropped out and need some help to aid you in getting back on track and perhaps getting a GED, call me right now at 404-542-3808. I can help you and put you in touch with others that can help you.

The Wise Men and Women told me that every human being is like a light bulb. They said that two male children were born on the same day at the same time in the same neighborhood on the same city. They said that one baby boy was born with the potential to shine at 80 watts. He went to the best schools but he refused to read or study to develop himself and although he had the capacity to shine at up to 80 watts he only ended up shining at 17 watts. The other baby was born with the capacity to only shine at 35 watts. He went to the worst school in the neighborhood but because he took the time to read everything that he could get his hands on, because he pushed himself hard to grow and to study – although he was only supposed to shine at 35 watts he ended up shining at 83 watts! The kind of young people you choose to surround yourself with help determine which one of those young men you will end up being. Whether you will ultimately end up shining at 17 watts or at 83 watts you must determine.

Every young man needs to run and get knowledge to put into his head. Stop being a lazy, trifling young man. Stop trying to look like and be like everybody else at your school. If there is one complaint that I have about your generation it is that nobody seems to want to be different. The Creator of your life had a specific design and pattern for your life in creating you in the way that He did. The wise men and women have taught me that people often say that this or that young man has not yet found himself. However, they also taught me that the self of any young man is not something that they can find but it is something that you have to create. This is why you need to get the right kind of education. Many educational professionals are doing the best they can to educate our young men with what they were given. But if that isn't working then what's the alternative? The word education comes from a Latin word, 'Educera', which means "to bring out of". Many educators have been taught that education is the process of putting something into the child. That is partly correct. Education is that which goes in but it goes in to bring something out of the child. Education is supposed to go in and connect with what the Creator has already put into the child of His talents and unique characteristics. But what is coming out of many of our young men today? Education is supposed to help cultivate you. Education is supposed to help civilize you. Education is supposed to refine you as a young man. The wise men and women have said that the ultimate sign that you have been truly educated is when you are able to make a contribution to the larger society. Maybe that is something for educators to consider. If so many of our young men aren't making any contribution to the society but are in fact destroying the society then maybe there is something wrong with what we are teaching our young people and particularly our young men.

Answering the **"Who am I"** question will tell you what special assets and capabilities you have. The most difficult thing in life is to know you. Each one of us is unique and incomparable. Your self-image is a composite – a montage – of all the mental pictures you have taken of yourself. All your life you have taken mind pictures of how you behave as a family person, what your parents, teachers and associates think of you, your past successes and failures, the physical appearance you project, and what will happen to you if you take a certain action such as speaking in public, tackling a new assignment, or joining a new group.

What happens when a young man has a positive self-image? When a young man has a positive self-image he has the following characteristics: He respects others and he respects himself. He knows that he is good and getting even better. He plays fair, and gives all he's got to his family, his school and to his community. A young man with a positive self-image makes good things happen and he is fun to be around. He assumes leadership positions, and sets a great example for others. When you have a positive self-image of yourself then you will like yourself a lot better. Young men with a positive self-image see themselves living a long, successful life.

What happens when a young man has a negative self-image? When a young man has a negative self-image and is convinced that he is second rate then he often harbors disrespect – even contempt for himself and others. He is afraid to stand up to the challenges of daily living and withdraws from helping others because he feels his efforts would probably be useless anyway. You need to know this. Young men who evaluate themselves negatively make up the masses of young men who fail or, at best, live in mediocrity. They endure a lot of dissatisfaction, defeat, and discomfort. They attract "bad luck", they know other people have it "in" for them, and regard their world as a prison they must live in until they die. Think of the **low** messages you are receiving from rap music today. **"Trap or Die"** or **"Get Rich or Die Trying"**. What is that? You just got onto the planet a few days ago and they are already trying to convince you that you don't have any options for your life outside of 'trappin'. You may go along with that if you have a negative self-image. The ignorance and lies keep on coming at you. **"You know we Trap all day, play all night. This is the life of a go – getta"**. It doesn't sound like your getting much of anything with those lyrics except more ignorance and death. One of the most unfortunate things about this particular song is that this is coming out of the mouth of a man that once was saying, **"I believe I can fly."** Think about some of the other rap lyrics of some of our rappers and entertainers. Many of them are saying every outrageous, salacious, scandalous and misogynistic thing that their minds can think of on their various Cd's. They are saying these things with huge crosses around their necks. In other words they are saying that I am a Christian or at least I am claiming Christ but I am promoting 100% filth and indecency in his name. Is this what Christ is all about? Have you ever considered why death, murder, killing, sex, drugs and alcohol are such a heavy part of rap music? You talk about a combo. Every fast food joint you go to has a thousand combo's for you to eat from. The real combo that many young men are selecting from is not from the fast food restaurant. It is a combo from a sub culture that is whittling away at your mind, heart and spirit each and every day. Why is it that every song that you hear must contain a few of the above-mentioned elements to get airplay? Whose airwaves are they anyway? Much of the music that's played in today's times fuels the negative self-image that young men have about themselves. Here's a dude out here trying to tell you that, **"He's a real, full blooded goon."** And all over America when I go out to conduct workshops, the youth tell me that they now are goons. The wise men taught me that you don't have to condemn a dirty glass. Just hold a clean glass up besides it. So I asked the **"young goons"**, did they know what the definition of a goon was? And just as I figured, they didn't know. So I shared with them that according to the dictionary, a goon was a thug hired to intimidate or harm opponents and a goon was also a stupid or oafish person. I then proceeded to tell the young goons that the first time I ever heard of a goon was during episodes of the cartoon, **"Popeye"**. They had a cartoon character named, **"Alice, the Goon"**. And the next time I heard the term goon was when I would watch Mafia movies. The Boss in the movie always needed people to do his dirty work. So he hired him some real goons to work for him. The boss would say, **"Tommy, Bobby, come here! I've got some work for the two of ya's over on the East Side. Jimmy's not paying up."** One of the goons would say, **"We'll take care of it boss."** The other goon might say, **"But boss, Jimmy doesn't have the money."** The boss might walk up to that goon and punch him in his nose and say, **"When I want your opinion, I'll give it to ya!"** Do you see why a goon is defined as a thug hired to intimidate or harm opponents or a stupid or oafish person? Goons don't call the shots; the shots are called for them. They are not the brains of the operation; they are just the muscle for the man who is the brains of the operation. My question to you if you are indeed a goon is, **"Who's calling your shots? Who is the brains behind your operation"** All you need to do is look at who is benefiting from young men acting out and rebelling against their parents.

Whatever you input into your brain is what you are going to output. Many young men are outputting, singing and walking up and down the streets quoting negative, destructive rap music as if that is the gospel truth. I see them with their headphones on in school, at church, in museums, on field trips and some of them even play their music in the restroom while they are sitting on the toilet. Some of them go to sleep with the music in their ears. You may not realize it but you are being indoctrinated into a 'deathstyle' and not a lifestyle. Death is absolutely riding into your conscious and subconscious minds through slick beats and rap lyrics. Young men with a negative self-image see themselves living a really short, unsuccessful life. It's a sad thing to read the obituary of a young man who has died or was killed and it's only 2 lines or so.

I am very sad to report that many of our young men don't have a clue as to who they are. I'm sure by now that you have heard a song on the radio or seen the video by the singer, John Legend, called, **"Ordinary People"**. The main chorus of this song says,

"We're just ordinary people / We don't know which way to go / Cuz we're ordinary people / Maybe we should take it slow (Take it slow oh, oh, ohh).

Well after giving those lyrics some thought I wanted to help you to see deeper into them. Ordinary people do ordinary things. **You have to understand that you may have been born to an ordinary woman and father but you ultimately came to them from an extraordinary Creator.** I wish that you really were into studying your Creator. He is known by many different names but we all come from one Creator. If you want to know yourself and who you are more fully you should take time to study the Creator that you come from. He is truly worthy to be studied! You come from a wonderful God! I have learned to love Him so much for everything that He has permitted me to see and to learn. I now know for sure that He loves me as a young man and has been with me all the days of my life and the same is true for you. **The wise men and women have shared with us that every male is genetically programmed to become a master of the universe.** I want you to read that again! Each one of us is programmed genetically to be a master of the universe. Our Creator has never made a mediocre anything. He didn't make a mediocre tree, or a mediocre bee, or a mediocre flea. Everything that God, the Creator, brought into existence is perfected in its evolutionary stage of development. In the Scriptures, He says that man and woman is the best of His creation. We are greater than the sun, the moon, the stars, the mountains, the rivers. We are greater than all that we can see, and even what we can't see. Man is called, not a glory of God, but the glory. The definite article, the glory of God, is man. Every one of us is potentially the glory of God! What does that mean?

How are you greater? The sun can only do what the sun does, and that's a lot, but the sun serves us. We draw from it light, life and energy. We are made up of fire as well as water. The fire of the sun is in each one of us. The sun, as the wise men and women has taught us, gives everything its color. It's powerful. But the sun is not the glory of God. Mount Everest, the tallest mountain on the earth, will astound you when you look at it, but it is not the glory of God. The sun doesn't think, Mount Everest can't think. The great waterfalls of Niagara, Victoria Falls, Zambezi Falls are all magnificent, but they are not the glory of God. Study the beauty of rocks in their magnificent colors. Not one of them is the glory of God. **The Creator of everything in existence has declared that you young man, young beloved brother, young gang banger, young thug, young dro, young nappy head, Weak lookin', slow lookin' boy, Dirty white sock on your toe lookin' boy, that doesn't think too much of yourself, you're the greatest of His creations.** Why? Because out of the mind of men and women can come a whole new heaven and a new earth. This is why man is called the glory of God, and this is why Scripture teaches us, **"As a man thinks in his heart, so is he."**

Asking yourself who you are is really a great question. It is the most important question you can ask yourself in your lifetime. It is sad but true that many young men have never had a real, substantive relationship with anyone. Some are empty mentally and psychologically. Some are empty financially. You can't run your life on empty. You have to understand that you are multi – dimensional. There are several aspects that I would like to better acquaint you with in this chapter. There is a great **spiritual** aspect or dimension to you. There is a **physical** dimension to you. There is an **emotional** dimension that is developing within you. There is a **mental** or **psychological** aspect to you. There is a **financial** or **economic** dimension to you. There is a **social** aspect to you. There is a **sexual** aspect to you as well. Let's get into this!

3a. Spiritual Dimension – Who are you becoming spiritually?

Who are you allowing the privilege of helping you to develop your moral character? Who is helping you to develop the inner you? Who is developing your soul? How much of your time is spent in the cultivation of who you really are? What is your attitude in these matters? Nowadays young men spend hours in front of the mirror concerned with how they look physically to the world but are not aware of how they look spiritually and morally to their Creator. Do you know your Creator? Who is He to you? Do you know how to pray or make contact with Him? The wise men and women have taught me that if it were not for our prayers, the Creator would care nothing for us. You might be the type of young man that prays every now and then. Maybe you have it like that with the Creator. I don't. I pray all the time. I need the care, the love and the unequalled guidance of the Creator every millisecond of the day. I need Him to help me to be successful with you and thousand of others who are each His unique and powerful Creations. One of the most important things that we could ever hope to receive from the Creator is His guidance. Don't pray for more Nike's, Addidas, and Reeboks. You can get those relatively easy by working for them. Pray for the Creator's guidance to get you safely through some rough years ahead. You will need His guidance to get you safely through the coming weeks, months and years of your life. Trust me on that. What you know will not be sufficient to carry you through. Many times you will go to churches or mosques or synagogues and not understand what's going on. That's natural. Don't walk away from religion because you don't understand. Just be patient and allow yourself time to grow in the knowledge, wisdom and understanding. To know God for yourself, in His Supreme reality is the most important thing that you will ever do. If young men grew physically at the rate they grow spiritually, many of them would spend their lives in a playpen.

When you truly know the Creator of us all then you would never be carried away over any other human being no matter how powerful they appear to be. Always know this, the real Power, the eternal Power, is with God. You must come to know God, not from your mother or fathers experience, but from your own life experiences as He delivers you from one difficulty after another, one trial after another. After you rely on Him and He delivers you, then you become more certain, and from that point on there is a change in you. And sometimes that change is brought about by a painful experience that shows you your true relationship with God and how helpless you truly are without him. There are many things that God is going to actively permit you to face in this world. In one religious Scripture I was reading, God was saying that He has created man (and woman) to face difficulty. It is a general law of nature, that as night follows day, likewise, ease follows difficulty. All religious texts teach human beings that struggle is ordained for man by God. When we face difficulty, we struggle; we are forced to turn to the God for help. The wise men and women told me to tell you that each time we turn away from the struggle to overcome difficulty, there then is deterioration of character and there is destruction of the Will -- and the Will that is within you is God's gift. It is His Essence that He gives to man and anything that deteriorates your Will destroys your ability to cope with the problems of life. Struggle is ordained. The exertion of energy in facing and overcoming difficulty strengthens character. Each time we face difficulty and use our faith in our Lord to overcome it, there is a reward. This reward gives us the incentive to try and try again. God sends us the storms to prove that he is the only shelter.

The wise men and women told me to remind you that God can take the place of anything, but nothing can or should ever take the place of God in your life. He will still be who He is without you or me. God can do without us, but we cannot do without Him. You would become wise if you were to ask God to be your teacher. How could you worship an all wise God and still be a fool? Another reason that you need to understand God better is that it will help you to keep things in balance. It's so easy to become caught up out here. I can promise you that you may end up in some pretty dark places where there will seem to be no light. My mother used to warn all of her children that, **"Whatever you do in the darkness will come to the light."** Just remember that God is with you in the darkness just as surely as He is with you in the light. *You may have already realized that you have a dark side to you.* The wise men and women have taught me that the dark side of each of us is very destructive. The music that you love so dearly is cultivating your dark side. There are things that we all do that we know belongs to darkness. That's why you and I rush to do those things in the darkness. For instance, when we want to lie, we don't tell our lies in the light (of truth). We tell it in the dark, where people who don't know the truth won't know what we are talking about when we lie. But when the truth is present our lies can't come out because our lies belong to darkness. All evil are things of darkness. And the things of darkness can't stand light because light exposes the things of darkness. Consider this: *What type of things would you do to others if you were sure that no one else would find out about it? What would you do to your own family members? What kinds of things would you be involved in if you were absolutely sure that you could avoid being found out?*

Now, if you look up in the sky at night you will see the moon. Did you know that there is a dark side to the moon up there? Have you ever even thought about why you never see the dark side of the moon? You don't see it because the Creator (God) keeps the bright side facing the earth, because we cannot plant or harvest by the dark side of the moon. Nothing can be nurtured by the dark side of the moon. It is only the bright side of the moon that reflects the light of the sun that is used in the nurturing process. Being in harmony with your Creator will help you tremendously. Even though you have faults, your harmonious relationship with the Creator will help you to keep your bright side in front of people. Your right and correct relationship with Him will help cover your faults.

3b. Physical Dimension – Who are you becoming physically?

I will say it again; the human being is truly the microcosm of the macrocosm. Our Creator has given the Universe a Sun, which is 93,000,000 miles away from the earth, and at the same time the Creator has given human beings a sun in their heads, which we call our brains. In case you didn't know, the nine planets of the solar system are Mercury, Venus, Earth, Mars, Jupiter, Saturn, Uranus, Neptune and Pluto. Did you know that the Sun is so powerful that her light strikes each of the nine planets of the Universe at their equator and causes each planet to spin on its axis at the terrific speed of 1,037 and 1/3 miles per hour. At the same time the Creator has given our brains nine systems of our body to rule. These systems include the Circulatory System, the Digestive System, the Glandular System, the Immune System, the Intestinal System, the Nervous System, the Respiratory System, the Structural System and the Urinary System. You have to choose to become more acquainted with what the Creator has put within you. With as much as young men tend to talk about girls it always amazes me how ignorant young men tend to be about the female anatomy. This ignorance is always preceded by a lack of knowledge of self.

Do you like the physical house that you showed up in? Are you pleased with yourself physically? Do you like your eyes as you stare into them? What about your nose? Do you like your ears, your mouth, or your teeth? Do you like your face and the way your head is shaped? There is this whole process of becoming acquainted with yourself that you have to become involved with. You have to start with the house you showed up in. You are not your body but you live in a body. Look at the body or the house that you now live in and occupy. Did you know that you have a responsibility to keep up your body? If you don't who else will? What physical hang up's do you have about yourself as a young man? I know I had plenty growing up. Children tend to believe most things that come out of the mouths of their mothers. When I was younger, I was consistently told that I was black and ugly. Since this came out of the mouth of my own mother I naturally accepted it. I did things to support my core belief that I was black and ugly. I used to literally run from the sunshine because I was told that the sun would make me blacker. One day I was told to go into the bathroom and scrub the black off of my face. So I went into the bathroom and got me a brillo pad and started trying to scrub this old ugly blackness off of my face. But of course it wouldn't come off. Then one day my mother shared with me, **"You are not ugly for nothing."** In other words, there was a reason why I was so ugly; I just hadn't discovered it yet. So many times people meet us and they don't know anything of our scars. The mean and harsh things that lighter skinned blacks and others have said to darker skinned blacks when they were growing up damage so many of them to this day. Many have told me that when they were little, their friends and family members would cut out all the lights in the house and then tell them to smile so that they could find them. One young lady shared with me that she would never want to have a baby with a dark skinned boy because she didn't want her baby to come out black and ugly. She said she didn't want a burnt looking baby. Even today many parents are relieved to look upon their newborn baby and find them to have an agreeable "light" complexion. I have begun the process of overcoming my old negative belief system about myself and I encourage you to get started. Many millions of our young men today are wounded and hurting on the inside. I accepted that I was physically handsome as a child, and that I am indeed a physically handsome man now. I had to accept that if I thought I was ugly, then how could I think well of the Creator that made me ugly? No the Creator didn't make a mistake with me and he has not made one with you. Human beings are the only creatures on the planet that are concerned with the physical appearance anyway. Could you picture our Creator rejecting a human being because of the way he or she looked? Could you picture the Creator of all human life being so shallow? Only a superficial, trivial, one - dimensional person is caught up in the way someone looks physically.

Now, you are going to have to get control over your body. You will have to learn about your body so that you will not abuse the magnificent house that you live in. The Creator has designed your body for you. It is a wonderful body but it is also extremely sophisticated. You are made in the Creator's image and after the Creator's own likeness. That should tell you that you have to study your own self in order to know something about your own Creator. You are not the image of an insect, a reptile or some sea animal. If you look carefully, you are in the image of a human being. The wise men and women have taught me that the Creator only differs from you in that He is absolutely supreme in knowledge, wisdom and understanding. You can become more and more like Him if you commit yourself to being a good student of His.

The frame of your body is only made to comfortably handle a certain amount of weight. As you get older it gets easier and easier for the weight to come on you and harder and harder to get it off of you. Our bodies become more and more taxed as we put on more and more weight. Many young men in America are overburdening their skeletal muscles with unwanted FAT. Bone, muscle, tendon and ligaments are designed to work together in a harmonious relationship to move the body. When we stand, our entire weight is carried by the power of our legs down to our feet. If taxed by excess weight, muscle wears down and eventually falters.

There is a precise, mathematical relationship between our skeleton, height and weight. Like the bones, the skeletal muscles range in size and shape to suit the particular functions they perform. Their ability to perform with speed and power can be literally of life-or-death importance, enabling us to move in response to sudden danger. When it is not overburdened, skeletal muscle can move into action within a few hundredths of a second and, when necessary, support 1,000 times its own weight.

My father was 6 feet 4 at 19 years old and weighed approximately 190 lbs. Twenty four years later he died at 44 years of age weighing nearly 450 lbs. He died from complications from a heart attack. The heart tries to keep up with our overeating but in the end it always loses. Your heart is one part of the circulatory system that includes blood and blood vessels. Your heart is the pump that pumps fluid through sixty thousand miles of veins in your body, and in mine. This perpetual pump rests and pumps, rests and pumps, that's how important the heart is. On many occasions, I witnessed my father struggle to walk up a flight of stairs. He would start sweating profusely. You might be skinny right now but that doesn't mean that you are healthy. Some young men are empty physically. They don't have any stamina. They don't get any vitamins from the food they eat because they live off of fast food. The wise men and women have sent me to tell you that fast food equals fast death. You can't survive off of McDonalds, Burger King, Checkers, Chinese Food, Taco Bell, Captain D's, White Castle's, Pizza Hut, Wendy's, Church's Fried Chicken, and certainly not Kentucky Fried Chicken and other assorted fast food merchants.

One way to keep up your body is not to abuse it with drugs, alcohol, cigarettes or weed. I regret the day that I started smoking. One of the main reasons I have never drunk alcohol is because I had a neighbor to be my example of why I shouldn't drink alcohol. Again, study people carefully. My neighbor used to be drunk most days by 8:00 a.m. He would guzzle down a bottle of Colt 45 as I was headed off to school. Then he would belch very loudly and tell me to have a good day at school. **Have you ever considered what's in a Colt 45?** Why doesn't Colt 45 have any ingredients on the label? What are you really drinking? While I appreciated his encouragement, I wished he had stopped drinking. He died of liver problems just a few short years later. If you abuse alcohol it will kill you as well. You must never turn to alcohol to drown out the problems of your life. I don't care how heavily rap music promotes drinking and sipping on some syrup. You must not allow alcohol to gain a foothold in your life. Once the wise men and women taught me that my body was my temple, I stopped smoking immediately. Now I understand the impact that putting that foolishness into my body has caused.

We are natural to the earth so we should try to put good and natural things into our bodies. Young man, what you are doing to your body as you light up these cigarettes is painful to bear. The wise men and women told me that the cigarettes have a light on one end but a fool on the other. Most young people who smoke cigarettes like a certain brand of cigarettes. Young men and women are more likely to smoke mentholated cigarettes like Newport's, Kools, and Salems that are very high in tar. Now what you may not know is that mentholated cigarettes are particularly dangerous because the smoke is pulled deeper into your lungs. With each puff that you inhale, at least 4,000 different chemicals enter into your body. Now here's what you really aren't thinking about. If you smoke and you are a drinker at a young age, have you forgotten at the same time you are producing sperm? This sperm will one day be the future of you and the future of life on the earth. You are producing a sperm that is already deficient. You are producing a sperm that is already deficient and this deficient sperm may contact a deficient egg in some female that is not healthy.

Look at your family's history. The wise men and women taught me that in the old days, if a parent 'just had' to smoke they would go out in the back of the house where they couldn't be easily seen. Folk's back then respected each other a little better. The minds and the hearts of children were more respected as well. Nowadays many parents smoke cigarettes, blunts, and drink liquor right in front of their children. This is a shameless day and time we live in. Have you ever thought about why some of the men in your family only lived to be 40 or 50 years old? It's because they were drinkers and smokers. And some of them were dead before you ever met them. What kind of men have been in your family? Do you like the legacy of what's been passed down to you? If you do, how will you continue the legacy? If you don't like it, how will you break the pattern? Are you the one or do we need to look for another? Will your children ever really know you? Will you be dead before your children or grandchildren arrive on the planet?

You have to learn how to fast as a young man. Not only will learning how to fast be good for your weight but it will help you to strengthen your own personal discipline. Fasting may be a new thing to you but it is certainly not a new thing in the world. The wise men and women have taught me that many people are learning the trick of curing their colds, headaches, nervous spells and other acute troubles by missing a few meals or taking a short fast. It is the simplest and the most efficient way of relieving the overloaded and "food-poisoned" system. You would be surprised to know how little food is actually required to keep you healthy. You will never need three meals a day to maintain your life. Eating that amount of meals a day will actually shorten your life because of the amount of poison that is in the food nowadays. The Wise men and women pointed out to me that **the doctors who prescribe for us to eat three or four times a day don't live any longer than their patients.** One of the most common complaints sick people have is that they have **"lost their appetite".** In fact, the greatest blessing to them would be to lose their appetite long enough to find their hunger.

Loss of appetite is an indication that our bodies system is overcharged with **toxins.** Nature is trying to correct this by giving the waste that has accumulated in your organs time to escape from your system. Fasting is a principle that actually helps to reform the conduct of man when it is practiced. We are creatures with desires and basic human needs like food, shelter, and love. We need to be respected in our community. We have a hunger for love, and for expressing our own being. All of these hungers, all of these needs, must be disciplined and controlled if society is to be successful. **You cannot escape discipline.** Whenever a human being lacks discipline, then you can observe that lack of discipline in the manifestation of excesses: excessive eating, excessive drinking, excessive sex, and striving to get more and more material things. The wise men and women have sent me to tell you that the first law of the Universe is motion. After something is put into motion, the second law is order. That which is in motion must come under order. This order presupposes discipline. And when there is no discipline, there is no order, and soon whatever motion you have will be brought to an end. That's why you must learn to fast. It will help you to put yourself under order. The wise men and women have shared with me that the Creator has a very powerful reason for asking us to give up food for a certain period of time. It is natural for you to eat and most people love to eat! **If you could give up a very natural thing like eating then what unnatural thing could you not give up as a result of your self-discipline?** What you see in our community today is the lack of self-control and self-discipline. The lack of discipline in our community not only leads to the untimely death of individuals but it is also leads to the death of the family and the society.

You have to take care of your teeth. Whatever you don't take care of now as a young man won't take care of you when you get a little older. One of the first things another person will notice about you is your smile. Your teeth are some of the hardest substances in your body. Your teeth are also necessary for chewing (or mastication) - the process by which you tear, cut, and grind food in preparation for swallowing. Chewing allows enzymes and lubricants released in the mouth to further digest, or break down, food. Without our teeth you'd have to eat nothing but soft, mashed food. Eating would not be quite as enjoyable! Proper dental care includes a good diet, frequent cleaning of the teeth after eating, and regular dental checkups. Some young men have never been to the dentist. Going to the dentist is essential to maintaining healthy teeth and avoiding tooth decay and gum disease.

You also have to take better care of your feet. Twenty five percent of the bones of your body are in your feet. If any of these bones are misaligned, your entire body could be affected. Did you know that foot problems could cause knee problems, hip or low-back problems, shoulder and neck problems and even headaches or stomachaches? Foot problems can also cause emotional stresses and physiological changes in the body like adrenal stress, blood sugar, fatigue and many others. Be mindful of the importance of wearing comfortable shoes. Make sure that they are not too tight.

I need to mention tattooing with you as well. You don't have to get a tattoo and you don't have to get your ears, nose or tongue pierced if you don't want to. This decorative art form continues to be a growing attraction to teenagers. It is reported that teenagers as young as 13 and 14 are getting their first tattoos. Some young men are so hard up to be 'in" and have a tattoo that they are putting them on themselves. Some are using regular needles. Some are using pencil erasers to do it. It isn't just guys who are getting them. Over the past twenty years the number of women getting tattoos has quadrupled. Remember, a tattoo is forever. Some people may think that it is a way to express their individuality. Some people see it as an art form. But before you walk into a tattoo studio, you should know exactly what you want to put on your body. Permanent tattoos are applied by injecting color pigments into the skin using a solid, round-tip needle attached to a motorized instrument that holds up to 14 needles attached to the pigments. The pigments are injected into the middle layer of the skin at a rate of 15 to 3,000 times per minute. Please be sure that this is what you want to do before you sit down.

3c. Emotional Dimension – Who are you becoming emotionally?

Some young men believe that males don't have emotions but that is not true. In fact, it is very stereotypical to think that males don't have emotions. Young men are taught from birth to suppress their emotions and to hide any feelings of fear, sorrow, or tenderness. Even as a small child, you were probably warned not to be a "cry baby." Now as a growing young man you have become very efficient at holding back tears and keeping a "stiff upper lip." Some young men don't even cry at funerals of loved ones they were close to. Instead of expressing any emotions some young men have simply learned to play the 'silence game'. The current generation of males has been silenced. Growing up in America is so difficult for young men that they are simply rendered speechless. Sometimes I greet young men with words and they greet me with a quick nod of the head. Some of them actually grunt at me. I say, **"Hey brother"**. He says, **"What's up dog!"** Do you see what's happening? Now young men are telling me that they don't believe in snitching. Some young men tell me that even if they saw someone kill another person, they aren't going to tell who did it. What is that but another aspect of the silence game? Most of our parents were never taught and trained in their own upbringing how to properly handle emotion. Many of them were the victims of neglect, or anger or rage coming up out of their parents. They may have never learned how to handle you properly. And as we are told, an abused child grows up to become an abusive parent. The same is true that a neglected child grows up to be a neglectful parent. Maybe your father wasn't in your life because he also was playing the silence game. Do you think his absence has had no real effect on your life? They say much of a son's training should consist of a father's example. When a father isn't in the life of his son how does the son process that? Some young men internalize their father's rejection of them. **You may have processed his rejection as an indication that you were not worth having a relationship with or not worth knowing.**

Every human being has a need to be known. When your needs are not met then your resentments grow and your silence runs deeper. The silence game can be very frustrating to a young man, not to mention the effect it has on others. Most of us know when we are doing it; few of us know how to stop it. **Why won't you talk? Why won't you express yourself more? Why won't you voice your opinion? Why are you not out front leading the way? Why won't you share you thoughts, your feelings and your ideas as a young man?** Being able to communicate with people is a powerful skill. Silence is a behavior some young men learn in order to protect themselves. In this society a young man is often penalized for thinking out loud. Most teachers hate an intelligent young man who can respond to them as quickly as they can ask the questions. Some young men often come across as cold and callous because of their silence. Some have learned that people can take advantage of them through manipulating their emotions. Young men are capable of expressing a wide range of emotions, but unfortunately they only allow themselves to do so in rare instances – like a game, for example. Young men's silence keeps them locked in and others locked out. **Why are you playing the silent game on your mother? Why are you playing it on your girlfriend?** We play the silent game for many reasons, but usually it is because we are upset about something. We can't or we won't communicate our feelings and we resent that others don't sense our needs, and then we shut them out. Some young men think that being silent makes them look cool and mysterious.

Loyalty to your image and to your silence demands a high price. I have learned that many young men are extremely lonely and they have a hard time opening up to people. Their silence no longer works for them, but against them. The problem is, most young men and grown men don't express their emotions. All you have to do is visit any hospital and see how many men are hospitalized for stress – related disorders such as heart attacks, stomach problems, or addictions. It is stressful being a young man, but even more so when you lack emotional expression.

It is true that you must work very hard to keep your emotions under control. It's the idea that you must repress yourself that I have a problem with. It is okay from this day forward for you to feel and to get emotionally involved. It will not slow you down at all but will enhance you greatly. So many young men have never had a real, substantive relationship with anyone. **Have you ever been in love as a young man?** The wise men and women have said that if you have love, you don't need to have anything else. If you don't have it, it doesn't matter much what else you have. I can tell you that love is magnificent and wonderful to have in your life. Many of you have felt something on the inside of your heart for a female. I would never tell you that you don't know what love is. I will share with you that your understanding of what love is all about will get deeper and become more thorough as you go on in life. I got my first real lesson in love when I was very young. *I thought I was in love way back when I was in elementary school.* I remember her name well. Her name was Carol. I 'lovded' Carol so much, or so I thought. I wanted to see if she felt the same way about me. So I wrote her a note one day. I asked her if she liked me, check the box marked, **"Yes"**. If she didn't like me, check the box marked, **"No"**. If she thought she might like me, check the box marked, **"Maybe"**. She got the note, giggled a little, wrote her response and sent me back her response. Now you know how a real playa had to do it. I raised my hand and asked the teacher could I use the restroom. The teacher agreed and when I got to the restroom I locked the door and went into the bathroom stall. I said a quick prayer and then I opened the note. It said, **"HELL NO, I DON'T LIKE YOU!"** Stop laughing at me. It's not funny. **The one thing no one ever shares with you is just because you love somebody doesn't mean they have got to love you back.** You cannot tell your heart whom to love. You will be surprised whom you may end up with as a life partner. Some of you as young men try to play like you are so hard. Maybe it was only after some young woman broke your heart that you began to proclaim to the world that you were indeed a pimp, a player or a hustler. Now you are out here claiming that you are a heartbreaker. Because someone wasn't careful with your heart you feel justified in not being careful with the heart of someone who truly likes you. Today it seems as if many teen relationships are about hurting someone else before they can hurt you.

Assuming you had a girlfriend, let me pose a few male / female relationship questions for you to consider. Some young men are way too possessive of a female. Please consider your answers to the following questions very carefully:

Are you a possessive young man? Yes _____ No _____

Do you believe that you own a female when you are dating her?
Yes _____ No _____

What responsibility do you believe a young man has to a young woman?

What responsibility do you believe a young woman has to a young man?

Do you feel jealous often? Yes _____ No _____

Would you be jealous of other people in your girlfriend's life?
Yes _____ No _____

Do you want her to only be with you? Yes _____ No _____

Would you constantly question her about her whereabouts, phone calls
and conversations? Yes _____ No _____

Do you feel you have the right to tell her what to do, who to talk to,
where to go and what to wear? Yes _____ No _____

Do you give her ultimatums? Yes _____ No _____

Would you make her chose between you and other things in her life?
Yes _____ No _____

Would you take your anger out on things in front of her?
Yes _____ No _____

Have you ever broken things, punched things, and thrown things when
you're angry? Yes _____ No _____

Have you grabbed, pushed, slapped, or hit a female when you were
angry? Yes _____ No _____

Do you blame others for your problems or your feelings?
Yes _____ No _____

If you ever hurt your partner would you blame them?
Yes _____ No _____

Do you make excuses for your reactions, especially if they hurt others?
Yes _____ No _____

Do you believe young men should be in control? Yes _____ No _____

Do you believe young women are inferior to young men?
Yes _____ No _____

Do you believe a woman is a man's property? Yes _____ No _____

So many young men believe that one day they are going to straighten up
when it comes to male – female relationships. The time to straighten up is
right now. Now is the time that you will learn how to be a decent man to a
young woman. Right now you should be thinking about the kind of female
that you want in your life. In fact, could you describe your ideal female?

Describing your ideal mate:

Should they be shorter than you? Yes _____ No _____

Should they be taller than you? Yes _____ No _____

Should they be smarter than you? Yes _____ No _____

How much education do they need to have?

_____ At least finished high school

_____ Some College would be nice

_____ At least a B.A. or B.S. Degree

_____ Must have a Masters or at least be actively pursuing it

_____ Nothing but doctors

Should they come from a large family? Yes _____ No _____

Should they be an only child? Yes _____ No _____

Should they be a flirt? Yes _____ No _____

Should they have already have money? Yes _____ No _____ How Much money?

__ a couple hundred

__ a couple thousand

__ a couple million

Should they like to travel? Yes _____ No _____

Should they like to stay at home? Yes _____ No _____

Should they already have a child from another relationship?

Yes _____ No _____

Should they be better looking than you? Yes _____ No _____

Should they be older than you? Yes _____ No _____

How much: _____ At least 3-5 years _____ At least 5 – 10 years

_____ At least 10 – 15 years _____ At least 15 – 20

Can they be a smoker? Yes _____ No _____

Do they need to know how to dance? Yes _____ No _____

Do they need to know how to cook? Yes _____ No _____

Do they have to go to church? Yes _____ No _____

Do they have to have all their limbs? Yes _____ No _____

Do they have to have all their teeth? Yes _____ No _____

Do they have to know how to drive? Yes _____ No _____

Is it important for your partner to keep up with what is going on in the world

Yes _____ No _____

How much should your ideal partner weigh? (Please shade in)

0 -100 lbs	101 – 200 lbs	201 – 300 lbs	301 – 400 lbs	401 – 500 lbs	501 – 1000 lbs

Most grown men never asked those questions before they got involved in their relationships. Remember to ask yourself all the questions you need to before you settle down with any female. **I would also recommend ordering my CD, "What are the questions you must have answered before you say I do?"**

3d. Mental / Psychological – Who are you becoming mentally and psychologically?

The wise men and women have taught me a great deal about this critical aspect of our lives. **They told me that your brain and your mind are two separate things.** Your brain is like the sun that controls the nine planets of our solar system. The brain controls nine systems in the body and these systems are only balanced well when the brain is filled with the energy of light and truth. Your brain can only grow to be so big but your mind can span the sum total of the universe, which is 76 quintillion miles. (A unit followed by 21 ciphers). Your mind is the sum total of your knowledge, wisdom and understanding. What creates your mind is how you allow God's creation to affect you. One of the names that God is known by in the world is, **"The best Knower."** You can't release the power that He has put within you without knowledge. The thing that separates us as human beings from the beasts of the field is that there is a hunger and a thirst in the human being for knowledge. And that's why in the first year of life a curious child learns to crawl. Parents don't have to tell the child to crawl. Where does that intelligence come from? Nine to ten months later, the child finds something strong and it pulls up; then it takes its first step. Again, a parent didn't have to tell the child to do that; something within told it.

Your mind is extraordinarily complex. Yet it works in a simple, three step way. First, it takes in information (what you see, hear, smell, taste, and feel). Next, it processes this information (how does what you sense relate to you?). Third, after processing the information, your brain tells you what action to take to handle it. In building a life of success or failure, your mind takes in information, processes it, and then consciously and subconsciously tells you what to do. Notice that whatever you do or say begins with information input or what you allow to get into your mind. What you input into your mind will indeed be what you output. A key step in achieving more in your life is to make sure the right kind of information is put into your mind for processing, which in turn leads to the right kind of action. You **have to protect your mind because it is your multimillion-dollar asset.**

In the United States it is estimated that one in twelve people will spend some time in a mental hospital. Let's assume that you own and have in your physical possession a million dollars in gold. Would you protect it? Of course you would, and with plenty of care. You might have electronic devices installed, hire guards, insure its safety, or take whatever action you feel is needed. Well your mind is worth far more than a million dollars. Your mind is the exclusive source of all you will create spiritually and materially in your life. Your level of happiness, security, contributions to others, your dreams, all come from one place – your mind. Most young men do not protect their minds as carefully as they protect their physical assets. Of all the things that the Creator ever gave you, your mind is His most valuable gift to you. Your mind is super powerful. Our minds are sacred. We have to begin to feed our minds a better quality of knowledge. If you eat cheap food, it corrupts your body. If you feed your mind filth, it corrupts your mind. They say, **"Man is what he eats."** And if you're feeding your mind garbage, then you become a garbage pail, and as a garbage pail, you won't produce anything but maggots and flies. No one can see what is in your mind until you begin to manifest some activity. Who wants to be around a person that's not doing anything?

The wise men and women have taught me that the brain of a young man is infinite. If the brain of a young man is infinite, then a young man can bring into existence whatever he conceives in his mind, good or bad. The Creator can live inside you or you can give the weaker part of you a place to rule from. Real power grows in you when you have knowledge in your head. Knowledge will enable you to leap over all the obstacles in your path, get under them, get over them, get around them, go through them, but its knowledge that you need. You also need somebody to come along and challenge you in the way you think. I hope this book is doing that for you. The doctors say a man is dead even if his heart is pumping, if he's brain dead. **So for your brain to be dead or when you say you are chilling as a young man what do you really mean?** The core of your brain generates thought, which is the life of the brain. The brain is what allows you to bring up vision, and where there is no vision for your life, you will perish as a young man. The best measure of a young man's mentality is the importance of the things he will argue about. Be careful what you argue about as a young man. We live in a day and time when people will kill you without any reason or cause whatsoever. This is why developing your mind is important. **This is why millions and billions of dollars are spent in America on how to manipulate the masses of people through the manipulation of their minds.** Who's in control of your mind right now? What goes on in the core of your thinking is sacred. What's riding your intelligence? Who's riding your intelligence? Is it life? Is it death? I ask young men in my groups that question. I ask them, **"Who in this room looks like a killer? Who looks like a murderer?"** They start looking around the room and they point at this one or that one. But the truth is that any one of us could be a murderer or a killer under the right circumstances. You can never tell what's in the mind of another human being just by looking at them. We look at each other everyday, but you don't know what that person is really thinking and he or she doesn't know what you're really thinking. Many young men have mastered the art of camouflage. Many young men are perpetrating a fraud when they go out. Some of us as young men haven't seen ourselves, because we have not been true to ourselves, and if you lie to yourself you'll lie to anybody. I am trying through this book to help you to look into the core of your thinking about yourself.

Our physical body requires food (nourishment) to stimulate and sustain it but so does our minds. According to the information that I read, the average man speaks four hundred words well. Do you know how important it is to have a good vocabulary? Did you know that it is estimated that **there are more than six hundred thousand words in the English language.** Did you know the current edition of the Webster's Dictionary contains at least 80,000 words? Imagine only knowing 400 words out of 80,000 and that most of the words were little words, like "go" and "stop" and "left" and "right'. **Could this be why you cuss and use bad language so much?** When we get angry we reach up into our heads for whatever intelligence is there to fire at the person we are angry with, and if all we can throw is 400 words, then I guess you already know what happens. Cussing is considered baby language when you grow in intelligence. The wise men and women taught me that baby language is that which only allows you to communicate with those in the crib with you. How can you have a relationship with a female if you know about 400 words and she knows about 400 words? That's only 800 words between the both of ya's? There are many people in America today who are in their homes grunting and gesturing at each other instead of speaking with each other. Maybe that's why so many young men are always walking around talking about, **"You know what I'm saying." "You know what I'm saying."** No, we don't know what you're saying! Did you know just saying that is a sign of incompetence?

Words develop the mind. Just as we must eat the right food to grow right physically: we must read right, from right material, to grow our minds properly. I was listening to a tape one day and the speaker said that he could tell how much money a man made in a year just by listening to that man speaking for a while. It's unfortunate, but here is an important fact. **People judge us everyday by the language and words we use.** Whether they are right or wrong for doing this, people make assumptions about your intelligence; your education and your capabilities listening to you speak. **Nothing makes a better impression than a solid mastery of the English language.** Studies over many decades have proven that a strong command of the English language is directly linked to your career advancement, to the money you will make and even to social success. To be successful in your career, your language and vocabulary level must at least equal the average level of the members of your chosen field. In fact as a young man, in order for you to excel in any business, your language and vocabulary must surpass that of your classmates. Not having a strong command of language can be a serious handicap. It is an obstacle that will prevent you from achieving your goals. Someone who cannot express his or her ideas eloquently, who hesitates because of uncertainty about the right word, can appear less than fully competent and qualified.

3e. Financial / Economic Dimension – Who are you becoming financially and economically?

Every young man has some financial needs. These needs will increase, as you get older. Every young man should quickly be able to distinguish between his needs and his wants. Knowing the difference between the two will help you tremendously. You need air, you need water, you need shelter and you need food. Most people spend so much time trying to get their basic needs met that they never even consider their deeper needs. It can be a weird time in the life of a young man that is truly on his way to becoming a man. He moves from being totally dependent to somewhat being independent. This of course depends on that young man's maturity level. I believe that every young man should have some markers that he has identified in his life that will help him to know for sure that he's moving solidly down that road. So many young men feel like their parents are somehow trying to hold them back from being the young man that they are supposed to be. I can guarantee you that when it is time for you to properly leave your home no one will be standing in your way.

Your home may seem like a jail or some place of confinement, but the only way you can leave any place that confines you is through own personal self-development. Getting ready to move out of your home is like you are being born all over. You have to see your home as a place of gestation, growth and development for you. **If you will grow and develop, then your home and your parents cannot justifiably hold you any longer.** But that's only if you grow. If you don't grow then you'll be twenty-five and then thirty-five, still living at home. In nature we witness the mother bird kicking the baby birds out of the nest. If they can't fly and make it on their own then something else in nature just eats them up. The way the Creator has constructed life on His planet is everything has to justify its existence on the planet. Many parents refuse to let their sons grow up. There is an old saying of how mothers and fathers raise their daughters and love their sons. There's nothing wrong with parents loving their son to a large degree but they can't live your life for you as a man. The wise men and women have taught me that the next stage after ripe is rotten. Our community is producing a great deal of rotten men. **You must get out here and struggle to overcome the adversities that are in this world just for you.** Young man there are certain things you will have to know to survive out here in this place called America. So here we go!

You should prepare to start moving for a whole year. You should make sure that your parents know your plans. You should already have some means of employment before you start out. Do not sit and wait on anyone to give you a job, go out there and make a job for yourself! Try not to ever be the kind of young man who is waiting on someone else to make something happen. **Learn how to make things happen for yourself.** If you don't know how to do that, you just need to find a 'make it happen man' and follow behind him for a while. You need to develop your work ethic. Don't be a sit around kind of dude twisting your silly hair all day! While you are waiting for a job you should work. Work in the community and work for the community. **You should rake leaves, wash cars, and be willing to do whatever it takes to bring home honest, legal, and legitimate money.** Get on that legal grind daily for yourself. Remember that it is the daily grind that gives a person polish. Don't become involved with anything or anybody who could put you or your life in jeopardy. There's absolutely nothing wrong with working for someone else as long as you have the mentality that you are there to learn everything the boss knows. Make sure you have a big dream for yourself. I love to hear a young man with an ambitious plan and an ambitious dream. I love to meet young men who have the stamina and the energy that I know it's going to take to make it out here. My mother used to play a song on the record player when I was growing up called, **"God bless the child."** This song has verses in it that proved to be prophetic for me as I grew older. Some of the verses of this wonderful song go something like this:

"Money, you've got lots of friends
Crowding round the door
When you're gone, spending ends
They don't come no more
Rich relations give
Crust of bread and such
You can help yourself
But don't take too much

Mama may have, Papa may have
But God bless the child that's got his own
That's got his own"

There is a scripture in the Bible that teaches, **"The fool and his money are soon parted."** There is another scripture that teaches us that, **"The borrower is the servant of the lender."** Always strive to get your own stuff! You will need to own everything that you will use. Purchase your own pots and pans, forks and spoons and knives. Purchase your own table. Purchase your own chairs. Purchase your own bed. Purchase your own night table or end table. Purchase your own towels. Purchase your own car from an auction versus buying it from a car dealership. This way, you will own your vehicle straight out instead of making payments on it for the next seven years. Do you really need to follow the foolish trends of other young men and paint your car the color of Cheetoe's, or the colors of Now-a-laters? They don't get a check from these companies for doing that to their car and you won't either. **Don't be a fool!** You don't need to spend more money on the rims than you did for the actual car. **An easy way to become poor is to pretend you are rich.** The only purpose for transportation is to transport you from point A to point B. You are supposed to drive your car, not live in your car. Where will your car transport you? Do you really need such a loud stereo system? Do you really need a DVD player in the car on the front dashboard? Our aim should be to become the most civilized young person we can be. It is the uncultured and uncivilized young man who wants you to hear the music coming out of their car five blocks away before they get there. It is the uncivilized young man who is not mindful of his language around his elders and women. **Act with some dignity and self-pride and for God's sake pull up your doggone pants!** Purchase your own insurance for your vehicle. Don't put that expense on your parents. When you mature your duty is to take as many of the expenses your parents were providing for your upkeep away from them so they can put it back into their pocket. Don't borrow anything from anybody if you can help it. If you fall on hard times don't ever take your car title to any Title Pawn like place ever. These places are diabolically wicked and 1000% rip-offs. Don't ever rent from the Rent A Center or other places like that if you can help it. If you don't have enough money to outright purchase it, then don't get it. It is so sad to watch those guys have to come and take someone's rented couch, refrigerator or computer just as they were about to sit down for the evening because they haven't paid their bill. Don't ever gamble with your hard earned money. **Pay for everything you purchase completely so you will own it when you close your door at night.**

Please do not go out here and mess your credit up with 5 or 6 credit cards. That was one of the worst mistakes I ever made. Credit card companies will give you a credit card even if you don't have a job! They know exactly what you are going to do with the card, shop until your credit limit goes pop! A little **$500** credit card limit can end up costing you **$4,000** or **$5,000** dollars to finally pay it off. If you don't pay them they will wreak havoc in your life. These people are financial gangsters. You haven't met a gangster until you had to deal with a title loan or title pawn place. Banks call them "personal" loans because if you miss a payment they get personal about it. The interest they will charge you is completely outrageous and they do it all with a straight face. The wise men and women told me that you're robbing yourself—and your future. Instead of funding your dreams and the life you deserve to live, your hard-earned money goes to fill the lender's pockets. Wouldn't it be better if the money you pay in interest could go into a savings account to help you reach your goals? Paying for everyday items by going into debt limits your choices because you're constantly caught paying for yesterday instead of moving toward tomorrow. I hasten to tell you that your future employers will be checking your credit before you can get the job. Don't waste your money in the lottery. Invest your money wisely. Remember before you move in with somebody else that it is best to have your own. It is easier to go in with people on things that you will both mutually need and will both mutually utilize as you both mature. However, at first, it may be to your advantage to get your own stuff.

One of the most important things that I can share with you in this whole book is how to handle money. You may not realize it but everything we have talked about is connected. Your finances will improve as you improve morally, spiritually, emotionally and psychologically. I know that you need money right now. How are you going to get it? My question to you is, **"Do you have a plan to get money legally and honestly?"** When I was younger, I grew up in Brooklyn, New York around a lot of drug dealing. I grew up around a lot of guys who were making fast money. Many of them are dead or in prison right now. You can't walk around in a daze. Open your eyes and see what the Creator is showing you. After seeing how things went down with those other young people I decided that I didn't want any sheriff or police officer crashing through my door with some "no knock" policy at 3:00 a.m. in the morning. I have no desire to hang around or be seen with drug dealers or users. So the wise men and women recommended that I choose the legal route. That was what I chose. You may be thinking another way. Many persons tune out the voice of conscience when money begins to talk. No young man can truly become a man asking somebody else for money all his life. **You need to get a job right now.** Then you can stop asking your folks for money and start requesting loans. Many adults believe that by the time the average teenager is able to work, he won't. If you don't have a job then you need to go and get one. Here are some rules that I have learned the hard way to live by when it comes to employment.

1. **"A check is better than no check at all."**
2. **"Don't let somebody else talk you out of a job especially when they are usually unemployed themselves."**
3. **"Never quit a job unless you have another one to go to tomorrow morning."**
4. **"You've got to start someplace."**
5. **"Working is one of the best medicines known to man / woman."**
6. **"Never keep friends around you who only know you when you've got money and something to give them."**

Let me continue being honest with you. There is nothing like working for a living. There is nothing like working for a period of time and then receiving a check for your labor. You may be wondering, **'Why do we have to work?'** The answer is that people work for money that they use to fulfill basic needs like food, shelter, etc. They also work to afford the extras in life that they want like vacations. We call this making a living. You have to be psychologically and emotionally prepared for such a move. A young man needs to be spiritually prepared for such a move. You will have to be socially and economically prepared for that move. Many young men attempt this move but have not prepared for this monumental move. **What you have to do is become very clear about the fact that one day you will have to experience what it is like to go out into the world and <u>pay your own way</u> and <u>take care of yourself.</u>** We call this independent living. You have to know and understand that you are totally expected to go out into the world and take care of yourself. In the very near future, there will not be any public assistance programs for anyone to be on. Public assistance was certainly not created for a young man's benefit at all. Let's look at how much money you will need to enjoy the life that you want just starting out.

"Let's take a look toward the future"

What kind of home do you want to live in one day? (Please check one)

Trailer _____   Apartment _____   House _____

Mansion _____   Boat _____   Motor home _____

Items that have to be Budgeted for	You should expect to pay this amount Monthly
Housing: Money for at least a two bed room / 1 bathroom house or apartment in a **decent** neighborhood…	**$400.00**
Electricity Bill: Money for all the lights, electricity, gas, air conditioning and the heating that you like to enjoy.	**$150.00**
Phone Bill: Money for the House Phone	**$100.00**
Cell phone: Money for a phone that you travel with to quickly get in touch with and be called by people important to you in case of emergencies.	**$70.00**
Cable / Satellite Bill: Money for **legal access** to dozens of cable stations so you can enjoy your life a little more and see what is happening in the world…	**$70.00**
Your Car Note: Transportation to get to the places you want to go and people you need to see…	**$300.00**
Car Insurance – Money for that little piece of paper that legally allows you to travel around…	**$150.00**
Gas for the Car – Money for Getting back and forth to work etc, etc…	**$100.00**
Car Maintenance – Money for Window Wipers, Oil Changes, Tire Changes and keeping your car clean…	**$50.00**
Food: Money to keep food at your house and food you have to purchase on the go… **$15.00 x 31** Days	**$465.00**
Other Household Items: Money for Cleansers, Detergent, Soap, Dishwashing Liquid…	**$100.00**
Clothing Expense – Money for Clothes / Uniforms for work, religious activities, social functions and around the house. Include in this money for shoes, jewelry and other accessories…	**$100.00**
Grooming / Hair Care / Nail Care: Money to get and maintain a polished and professional appearance….	**$100.00**
Miscellaneous Expenses: Internet Expenses, Traveling Expenses, Magazine and Book Expenses,	**$100.00**
Sub - Total:	**$2,255.00 – Approximate Bills a month** **$2,255.00 X 12 months = $27,060 a year!**

Reality Check (Let me break this down for you):

Let's say you got a job that paid you **$15.00** an hour. Many would say that's a real good job.

Then let's say you worked an average of **40** hours per week

Then **40** hours a week **x $15** an hour a week would mean you would earn **$600.00** a week

$$\begin{array}{r} \textbf{\$600.00} \text{ a week} \\ \underline{X \qquad \textbf{4}} \text{ weeks in every month} \end{array}$$

Means you make **$2,400.00** a month

$2,400.00 a month X 12 months = You're grossing about **$28,800.00** a year

But there is one problem. You might have forgotten about taxes:

Deductions / TAXES – When taxes are taken out, all workers have federal, state, Social Security (FICA), and Medicare taxes deducted from their earnings. Depending on where a person lives, he may also have local (city and/or county) taxes taken out. FICA and Medicare taxes are based on a percentage of a person's earnings. The more a person makes, the more he pays. Students might be interested to know that their employer pays for half of the total amount of FICA and Medicare taxes that the government collects.

So you might Gross **$28,800.00** a year
(The total amount you earn during a yearly pay period)
But you might only net **$23,000** a year
(Net pay is the total amount you are paid after deductions)

If you're only bringing: **$23,000** a year home
And your bills total: **$27,060** a year
You are running a deficit **$ -4,060** a year
You will need a second job just to make ends meet

Other things to consider like your habits and vices:
Do you smoke cigarettes? Yes _____ **No** _____
$4 a pack / A pack a week = $208.00 a year
$4 a pack / A pack a day = $1,460.00 a year
Do you drink alcohol? Yes _____ **No** _____
Do you have a drug habit? Yes _____ **No** _____
Do you have a club habit? Yes _____ **No** _____
Will you get credit cards? Yes _____ **No** _____
How much will you decorate your car?
A lot _____ **A little** _____ **Not at all** _____
How will you handle medicine? (There are approximately 40,000,000

uninsured Americans in this country right now.)

How are you going to survive? Get your finances right as a young man. There are so many people out here waiting to take all of your money from you. They love to see a young man coming into their store to spend $30,000 to $40,000 on some false teeth, I mean a grill! They love to see a young man coming to place $5,000 to $40,000 down on some spinners. A car **depreciates** in value as soon as you drive it off the lot. Depreciate means the value goes down. You might make it big one day. In one day you might go from being an unknown to the next day having a hit record. One day you might be poor and the next day you might have more money than you may know how to use. The first thing you might want to do is show off to your friends that you have money. So, you may start 'bling-blinging'. If you are not careful with the money that's coming in, you might be famous but you will also be broke. Many young men spend money for things they don't need to impress people they don't like. You may become famous but will you know how to handle your fame. Will your fame cause you to burnout? Life has to have real meaning to it. Many singers, rappers and entertainers today are very successful but their lives have no real meaning. How many cars can you own? How many things can you buy? Think before you go out there and hand anyone your hard earned money. Its not just about getting dollars but it's about getting the sense to go along with it. One immediate thing I would recommend to you is to get you a role model for your finances. Get somebody in your life that is making money and knows how to save some money. In fact get somebody for every aspect of your life that you are trying to master. Having that person in your life can save you years of pain and keep you from messing up your life. It's very easy to waste tens of thousands of your precious dollars in a relatively short amount of time.

If you notice, I didn't even include tithing or giving a portion of your money to charity. You should not be stingy with your wealth. If you are stingy with a small income, it's likely you won't be generous with a large one. Please don't only think about how you can benefit from every situation. Some young men think that everyone who attends church is just a bunch of hypocrites. Even if they are you should still give because giving is good for you to do. Giving is part of becoming a man. One of the marks that a person still maintains a child – like disposition is that they are always looking to receive. Some young men do whatever they do of good because they expect the recipients to do the same for them. One of the marks that a young man is developing a mature attitude is that he no longer looks to receive anything out of what he does. I wished that you honestly believed that it was better to give than to receive. If you don't believe that it may be because you are still a child. Children are always looking to receive something. Maybe you should live by this creed: If you want to get a lot, then you have got to give a lot. **A law that can't be repealed is, "To get, you've got to give."** The law applies in every profession, occupation, and business. The way to riches, wealth, and more respect is to put giving first, and let getting come naturally. The hand that gives is the hand that receives.

Learn to use money to your advantage. Remember that it's good to have things that money can buy, but better to have things money can't buy. One of the greatest lessons the wise men and women told me to share with you is to learn to live within your means. They told me that some young men don't think they are having a good time unless they are doing what they cannot afford. It is true that money can't buy everything – including what it used to. However if some money should come your way I believe that you should take it and put it in the bank. If you don't yet have a bank account, get one. Most banks will allow you to get an account with them for free. You need a bank account. After you get an account then you can get an ATM card. Have you noticed that even the restaurants accept debit cards from people? It's all about convenience. Many people don't even carry cash on them anymore.

3f. Social Dimension – Who are you becoming socially?

This is a very good question. I'm just keeping it real with you. I don't believe you should move out from under your parent's authority if you are not mature enough to do so. If you can't function properly under your parent's rules and regulations then you won't function well at someone else's house or even with your own rules. Many young men move out of their homes in rebellion against their parents. So many young men are angry because their parents have set down rules by which they will govern their home. There must be rules in the home, at school, at church and at the job. There must be rules that teach us how to relate to one another properly in these places. If there are no rules in the home that enforce respect for parents, for children, for self and one another then you will never respect the existing rules and regulations that will be everywhere else that you go on the planet. When there are no rules in your house, there will be no order. Chaos will be the result. Where there is chaos, it will bring to an end the activity or the life of the home, the school and the community. When you start to pay the bills for *your* home then you can choose whatever rules you feel are necessary to govern your home. It is at this time that you will see the necessity of these rules. **It is so hard on your parents to watch you rebel against them especially if they are telling you right.** Some young men cuss their parents;

some strive to even physically contend with them. I warn you: **You should never raise your voice or your hands to your parents.** You can learn to live in such a way that you never have to raise your hands to anyone out here. Your mother is your mother and your father is your father. They are not perfect and they didn't bring you into the world to judge them. You will only get one of each in your lifetime. Do you really think you will be blessed speaking to them in an ugly way? They brought you into the world. They produced you; you didn't produce them. If you cannot be grateful over anything that they have done then at least be grateful that they came together to produce you. **You wouldn't even be here were it not for them coming together during that time that they were together.** Displaying sincere gratitude is another distinguishing mark of a man. One of the worst traits that I sometimes find in your generation is the characteristic of ingratitude. An ungrateful young man is a person who doesn't have the maturity level to even acknowledge what others have given them in terms of their time, their talents, their money and resources in order for that young man to move further along in their life. Even if you feel like nobody has helped you recently in your life, what about all the other times when people went out of their way for you? The only people you should ever try to get even with are those who have helped you. The wise men and women taught me that gratitude is the heart's memory. In the very short amount of time your parents were together look whose life is now possible? So many young men have told me that their father doesn't mean anything to them. They tell me that their father has never done anything for them at all. That may be true. However I ask them, **"Are you any better than your father?"** It's easy for them to emphatically state, **"Yeah, I'm better than my father!"** But what's the proof? Just saying that you are better doesn't mean anything. I have learned to love my parents very much, especially my father. Maybe you are too close to your situation to appreciate your father. Maybe the hurt is too intense and too fresh for you. There is a saying that before you judge a man you should walk a mile in his shoes. I have now walked that mile in my father's shoes and then some. If he were still alive he would be worthy for me to carry him on my shoulders everywhere he wanted to go. I wish that you had a father that you loved like you claim to love your mother. Maybe you are not prepared at this time to handle the truth of why he really may have left your home. Many young men found out much later what the real reasons were. You might ask me did I grow up in a perfect house. No my brother. My house was as far away from perfection as the sun is from the earth. My house was extremely dysfunctional. But what does that mean? The prefix 'dys' comes from Latin and can be translated to mean pain. Functional means the ability to perform or function. When we talk about dysfunctional people, we are talking about people who are functioning in pain. Are they able to perform? Yes. Are they in pain? Yes. Was my father in pain? Yes! Was my mother in pain? Yes! Are your folks probably in pain as they try to prepare you for life? Yes! Will the pain ever end? Yessss it will.....one day! You won't get to sing Anthony Hamilton's song, **"Struggle no more"** just yet.

This society does not honor fathers at all. You will not feel the pain of that until you become a father. When Mothers Day comes around every year, you go to the mall you go into stores and you can hardly buy a card. There are no flowers left, there is no candy left. The restaurants are always packed to capacity. People cry as they try to express to their mother what she means to them. People travel across the country to be with their mothers on Mother's Day. Mothers are so worthy in this society. Father's Day also comes around every year. There are always plenty of flowers, plenty of candy and plenty of cards to choose from. Many sons will not even pick up the phone and call their dad on Father's Day. When a son doesn't have a father in his life, the son is placed in a vulnerable condition. That puts great pressure on a growing son. Millions of children do not know, and will never know, what it means to have a father. Many of them do not know anyone who has a father nor is a father. **Our boys are being destroyed because men are being neutralized in this society.** I go from group to group, organization to organization and rarely ever see a man in a leadership capacity. Many believe that men are just about useless in this society. You would be well advised to study the lyrics to Beyonce's song, "Irreplaceable":

Mmmm	to	the	left,	to	the	left
Everything	you	own	in	the	box	to	the	left
In	the	closet,	that's	my	stuff
Yes, if I bought it, then please don't touch (don't touch)

Now let's think about this. She recently sang this song. Evidently the young man in the song and Beyonce are breaking up. She is not advising him to get a U-Haul Truck to move his belongings. *She tells him that everything he owns is in a box to the left. Everything else in the house is what I bought with my money. Don't touch that! She says in the song, "Don't you ever get to thinking that you're irreplaceable!"* Be instructed by this young man... These young women today are a different kind of young woman. You've got to be up to par to get one in your life and you'd better stay up to par to keep one in your life. Just as a side note, Beyonce couldn't sing this song to me! She may indeed find another male to be in her life. But he wouldn't be me! After dating me I could guarantee her that she would never find the kind of heart, the kind of soul, the knowledge, the wisdom, the understanding, the love, the spirit, and the kind of passion that I would bring into her life. I am not a garden-variety type of man. You don't find men like me every day! And no woman should be able to find a young man like you on any corner she looks. You must come to view yourself as special and unique. Every male has to increase his mental, spiritual and moral capacity.

The moment you step outside of your doors of your home, you are in the public eye. How you interact socially in this world helps other people determine a great deal about you. Try not to be loud and obnoxious in public. Learn how to talk to people. The wise men and women taught me that a heavy sword will not cut soft silk. By using sweet words and gentleness you may lead an elephant with a hair. I don't believe that you should ever worry about knowing people – you should just make yourself worth knowing. To do that just consider how you are known right now as a young man. Every young man has to have people around him that will be honest with him. You will need people like this in your life for the rest of your life. Ask yourself these questions. **How do other people see me? What do they think of me? What have they shared with me that they see in me? Is it difficult to accept the truth about myself from other people? Who can I go to who will always tell me the truth about me?** How honest are you? No one knows of your honesty and sincerity unless you give out some samples. Are you a truthful person or are you just another beautiful liar? Do you tell beautiful lies and put lies together fantastically?

<u>**Take this little exercise to see:**</u>

There are a number of reasons why young men lie. The first is fear. They don't want to be punished for something they said or did.

Do you believe that it is okay to lie sometimes? Yes _____ No _____
Would you lie to escape punishment? Yes _____ No _____
If someone confronted you with the truth, would you still lie?
Yes _____ No _____
Do you lie by reflex? Is lying a habit for you? Yes _____ No _____
You have seen other people lie before? Yes _____ No _____
Have you known many adults who lied and got away with it?
Yes _____ No _____
If you were to tell the truth all the time would you get what you wanted?
Yes _____ No _____
Do you think that a young man who lies once in a while is the same as someone who lies all the time? Yes _____ No _____
Do you know someone who lies all the time? Yes _____ No _____

Do you like being around this person? Yes _____ No _____

How good of a liar are you? (Check all that apply to you)
_____ I'm the best there is
_____ I start laughing when I'm lying
_____ I can lie to anyone with a straight face
_____ I lie so much I don't even know when I'm telling the truth
_____ Lying is fun for me
_____ Don't trust anything I say
_____ I can't stop lying
_____ If I tell the truth I can't get what I want

Do you like being lied to? Yes _____ No _____Why or Why Not?
Do you hold others to a higher standard than you hold yourself?
Yes _____ No _____
Is it cool for your parents to lie to you? Yes _____ No _____
Why or Why Not?
Is it cool for your friends to lie to you? Yes _____ No _____
Why or Why Not?
Would you keep a friend that kept lying to you? Yes _____ No _____
Why or Why Not?
Don't you lie to your friends sometimes? Yes _____ No _____
Why or Why Not?

Under what circumstances is it cool for you to be lied to?

_____

Who must you lie to in your life? Who is above the truth?

_____ My Mother   _____ My Father   _____ My Grand parents

_____ My Principal   _____ My Friends   _____ My Boyfriend /
Girlfriend

You have to know the answer to these questions. No one is above the truth. I wish that you would believe that. Honesty is still the best policy. **The wise men and women have taught me that you can fool some of the people all of the time, and all of the people some of the time, but you can not fool all of the people all of the time.** They said that sometimes a young man could know the truth and not share it with others. They said that lying could be done with words and also with silence. They said that it is so easy to deceive yourself. If a young person wants something to be true they just have to believe it long enough. What are you trying to make true although you know it's false. It is much easier to be false or untrue in life. To be truthful and honest is very difficult and when a young person is in doubt, they should tell the truth. You should strive to always tell the truth. Then you'll never have to remember what you said the last time. If you do not tell the truth about yourself you cannot tell it about other young people. Oh, the tangled webs young men weave when first they practice to deceive.

The human eye is not made by the Creator to see inwardly but is made to see outwardly. It takes other people to be honest with you to help you see yourself. So a wise young man listens to the comments that people make about him. Other people hear things in you when you speak, observe things about you when you act and perceive you just as you are able to do the same to them and for them. As you talk, laugh and just try to live your life everyone who deals with you comes away with either a positive or a negative impression of you. Sure everybody has an opinion. It is wise to listen to all sides. No one is liked or loved by everyone. Do you mistakenly believe that your faults are somehow elusive and that people can't pick up on them? **We can't have true friends who will only tell us the things we want to hear.** Have you consistently heard the same things said about you or even similar things over a five or ten year period from your family, your friends, your co – workers and your various girlfriends? Don't you think that there may be the tiniest possibility that there is some truth to what they were kind enough to share with you? Every young man must search for the truth about himself, for the truth is not always on the surface. Maybe it's time that you asked for a good, honest critique from someone who has been around you for a few years. Most young men can't, and will not take or accept criticism from anyone and choose to live in a fantasy world where their opinion of themselves is the only opinion that matters. We have to remember that our perceptions of ourselves are only half of reality. Perhaps with more time and maturity we can sit and honestly hear how our words, actions and deeds have affected the people around us.

Other questions that you must ask yourself include:

Can you accept a compliment? Yes _____ No _____
Are you complimented on a regular basis? Yes _____ No _____
Who compliments you the most in your home?
Who compliments you the most at your church?
Who compliments you the most at your school?

Who always has had something nice to say about you?
Who has always had something negative to say about you?
Are you put down more than you are complimented?
Yes _____ No _____
Do you put other young people down more than you compliment them?
Yes _____ No _____
Are you very skilled at tearing other young people down?
Yes _____ No _____
If you wanted to, could you build another young person up?
Yes _____ No _____
Would you be described by your peers as a courteous young person?
Yes   _____   No   _____
Do you have good manners? Yes _____ No _____
Are you a rude young person? Yes _____ No _____
Do you have good table manners? Yes _____ No _____
Are you inconsiderate of others? Yes _____ No _____
Are you a selfish young person? Is your first thought, *"What's in it for me?"* Yes _____ No _____
Do you know how to sit in public? Yes _____ No _____
Do you know how to eat properly in public? Yes _____ No _____
Have you ever taken an etiquette training class? Yes _____ No _____
Now that you are getting older isn't it time that you learned?
Yes _____ No _____
Are you a greedy person? Yes _____ No _____ I'm just hungry a lot _____
Are you a beggar? Do you constantly beg people for their food, their money or their stuff? Yes _____ No _____
How easily are you tempted by others?
Not that easily _____ Very Easily _____ I'm not tempted at all _____
Would you be willing to steal to get what you want?
_____ You bet
_____ If I wanted that thing bad enough
_____ I am a thief
_____ I've never been caught stealing
_____ I have never stolen anything in my life
_____ I've stolen before but I will never steal again

I believe it is very important that since we are talking about this social aspect of you to also address the critical subject of friends. The wise men and women told me to share with you that birds of a feather still flock together. In other words, people will judge you by the type of friends that you hang around. Who are your friends? What kind of company are you keeping as a young man? What do the young people that you hang out with do? What kind of thoughts do they think; what kind of words do they speak; and what kind of actions do they involve themselves in? Have you taken the time lately, to evaluate the people in your inner circle that you call your friends? How big is your inner circle? What is the process by which a person earns such a glorious title as a friend in your life? Do you accept any and everybody as your friend? Are you seeking the science of how to choose confidantes in your life?

People bring out different sides to you. Some friends will absolutely bring out your good side. They will help you bring out the beauty of who you really are as a human being. Some friends will absolutely bring out your bad side. They will cause you to manifest the darkness of your soul. Some friends will bring out your wild side. We all have one. Certain friends in your life will cause you to walk that proverbial tightrope. They will have you drinking, smoking, doing drugs, and having illicit sexual encounters with girls you don't even know just to impress them. In mathematics we learn the principle that opposites attract. It is highly likely that you will have some friends in your life that are the exact opposite of you. If you are basically a good person then you will probably have at least of couple of friends that are basically bad people. People who are used to doing bad or mischievous stuff know how to not get caught doing that kind of stuff. The ones who get caught are the good ones who try to engage in doing bad or mischievous stuff. Do you understand? Many good young men are dead today for rolling with the wrong crowd. Many before you were even a thought in your mothers mind were dead and gone being at the wrong place at the wrong time. We lose them everyday in every city in America. Have you already been warned? **Are you right now allowing someone in your life to occupy a prominent place that your parents told you was not good for you to hang around?** My mother used to tell me that a hard head made a soft but. That still is true today. Many young men have been brought low in their lives because of their friends. I meet them in my Juvenile Justice classes all of the time. It is natural to have friends in your life as a young man. You just have to keep an eye on them. Every friendship that you have in your life is like a giant tug of war. Either you are pulling them to be more like you or they are pulling you to be more like them. The wise men and women taught me early in my life that if I wasn't able to bring the people up in my life then I should never allow them to bring me down.

As you move into the next few years of your life you are going to have to move around a lot. There are things that you have to learn that you will need to learn alone and by yourself. You can't have your boys everywhere you go. I don't care how tight you all have become as friends. You were not born with them and they were not born with you. The wise men and women have taught me that in order to be successful in today's times a young man has to break away from the crowd. That is so true. **If you can't let your friends and associates go to do what you have to do in life then you are probably going to fail in life.** You will have to learn to associate with the right people. Learn to pinpoint those people who can help you become successful. It's also wise to associate with them since they can help you get ahead. By the same token, it doesn't make much sense to cultivate the friendship of those who can do nothing for you. Why try to grow a crop of weeds? Your very first goal as you become a man is to find out – which people can help you most? There is nothing wrong with trying to befriend people who are beyond your current station in life. You'll benefit tremendously by saving time and energy when you concentrate your efforts only on those people who can help you achieve your goals. To devote your attention to anyone else is a complete waste of time! Strive hard not to waste time and energy on the wrong individuals. Never beg people for their friendship. **Always be a self – respecting young man.**

Never get so wrapped up in anyone that you just can't live or breathe without him or her. All my life I have watched young men of magnificent potential go down the drain because they were not able to let go of people who were bad for their lives. You have to be honest with yourself. Are you planning on being a success in life? If you are then you are probably going to have to let some of your friends go if you truly want to be a financial success, a spiritual success, or an emotional and psychological success. You should be willing to be let go by your friends if you are impeding their progress. There is always the possibility that their parents might believe that you are a bad influence on their son or daughter. When I was in high school I had a group of friends that I just knew we would be friends forever. When we graduated we swore we would keep in touch. Little did we know that new friends would replace old friends. And that's okay too. You should ask yourself as a young man, **"Has your desire for the continual company and acceptance of your friends kept you from striving to be the very best that you could be?"** I'm sure that you have heard about the crabs in the barrel scenario. That's the one where all of the crabs are in the bottom of the barrel. And all of the crabs are fine as long as they are at the bottom of this barrel. But then one day, one of the crabs gets tired of being or existing at the bottom of the barrel and says, **"I'm getting out of the bottom of this barrel."** The other crabs hear this declaration and instead of aggressively trying to help push the crab up out of the barrel, they instinctively begin to work hard to pull that crab back down into the barrel to stay with them. Once they have got the rebellious crab back down in the barrel with them, then they begin to attack that crab for wanting to leave the barrel. They begin to explain how good it is in the bottom of this rotten barrel. They begin to remind that crab of all of the good times that they have had together and the fun times that are yet to come. The reason the crabs do this is because they want to keep things as they are. *Those crabs are happy as long as all the crabs think the same way and do the same things - then no crab can be the example of another way to live or another way to exist.*

Maybe you've already experienced this. The little story of the crabs in the bottom of the barrel could represent how some of the people think in your high school, college or the city that you have lived in all your life. The crabs in the bottom of the barrel could also represent the thinking of some of your own family members. Oh, everything is so lovely in our families as long as you are agreeing and going along. But the moment you make up your mind to change direction, the moment you decide you want to accept a new way of looking at life, the moment you decide to change your attitude about things then you can expect trouble. And in many cases our family members can be huge obstacles in improving the quality of our lives. **The strange thing about this is whom the main opposition comes from in the family.** Sometimes you expect it from one person and it comes from someone you would never have expected. You should also know that the crabs in the bottom of the barrel could represent the very powerful thoughts that currently occupy your subconscious mind and the way you were raised to think and to feel about everything in life. If you notice, every time you have a good thought to want to better your own life, something comes up from right within your own mind to tell you it's not worth the energy; it's not worth the time or the effort. Maybe you just keep telling yourself to go along to get along.

We often hear people say, **"But we've always done it this way. We've always done it that way".** But how long is 'always' anyway? Five years? Ten years? Twenty years or even 50 years? You will have to learn to become more observant of the language that people will use to twist you into submission to **their desires** and **their plans** for your life. They may say, **"Everybody's doing this or that."** Who is everybody? There are billions of people living on the earth today. Do they really mean everybody is doing this or that or the people *that they just left* are choosing to do that particular thing? It may be helpful to you to strive to be more exact with what you are saying or are representing. Try not to exaggerate when you speak with people and try to understand that people tend to exaggerate when they talk. Are you a gullible young man? Do you fall for any and everything people bring your way?

How you behave and function socially is critical to your success. Always be mindful of how you conduct yourself when you are in public. Be mindful of the tone of your voice. There should be no yelling, cussing and swearing in public. If you have a radio and you're driving you should never blast your radio for the whole community to hear what you are playing. You should especially turn your radio down when you are driving through residential and business areas. When you are out in the community, strive to respect all people. Strive to be polite and courteous. Do not be loud and boisterous. Strive hard to keep yourself clean as well as the inside and the outside of your living quarters. Striving to master these things will help you to get along better with people. When you are speaking with people you should look them right in the eye. You should speak in a very steady and direct voice without wavering a bit. If something happens that you were not anticipating stay under control. Don't freak out and let your emotions take over. If a small thing has the power to make you angry, does that not indicate something about your size? We must learn to get along with people everywhere we go whether it is on social terms or in our family life. **Part of your success and happiness depends upon the attitude and actions of other people towards you.** This attitude is determined by our own attitudes toward other people. You can make your attitude towards others just about what you want it to be. Unsuccessful young men who do not get ahead have failed almost entirely because they didn't know how to get along with other people. Be conscious of the expression on your face. Do you have a war face? Are you always frowned up and scowled up? Are you always 'mean mugging'? The wise men and women taught me that when you smile, the whole world smiles with you. They said that it takes seventy-three muscles to frown and only fourteen to smile. No wonder grouchy young men are always tired. Life is like a mirror – if we frown at it, it frowns back at us; if we smile, it returns the greeting. Smiles and frowns are both contagious. It's all up to you how you want to infect the other person. A smile is a powerful weapon; you can break ice with it. Are your fists clenched? What does your walk suggest about you?

Strive hard not to act in anti – social manner. Anti means against. So when a young man acts in an anti – social manner then they are behaving in a way that is against this society. And this society moves to get rid of those who can't fit in and who refuse to come under control. You have to learn how to maneuver through this society in order to get where you are trying to go. You won't get there 'knuckin, buckin' and cussing' every step of the way. Let's look at some anti – social things that some young men engage in. Are you the type of young man who intimidates others through threats of violence? Do you have persistently unruly and intimidating behavior? Do you willingly damage private or public property? Do you bully other young men? Do you constantly refer to females in a vulgar and disgusting way? Do you keep up a lot of noise nuisances and engage in graffiti and vandalism? Do you use and sell drugs? Do you litter everywhere you go? If you have the above listed qualities and characteristics and don't yet possess the ability to get along well with others then this society says that you are acting in an anti – social manner.

Many young men have gotten to the place where they don't care how they are dressed, how they look, how they sound, or how they smell in public. One day I was dealing with this group of young men and I noticed a particular funk in the air. It was like a deep musty smell mixed with extreme body odor. And as I started addressing this, I was told by one of the young men that, **"Real thugs don't bathe."** And I told him that, **"If I have to smell like that to be considered a thug, then I don't want it!"** You have to bathe every day. And I mean it is one of the most wonderful and rewarding experiences that you can have. Put music on when you bathe or shower. **"Get crunk with the towel." "Get jiggy with the soap."** Get in the habit of being, **"So fresh and so clean."** Use some type of deodorant as well as a nice cologne or oil scent to complement your nice smell. You have to make sure that your teeth go 'bling bling' from them being so clean and not from the tarter hitting the lights.

3g. Sexual Dimension – Who are you becoming sexually? There are some things you definitely need to know about sex before you think you are ready for it. One of the first things you need to know is that everybody's not doing it as the media may subtly proclaim. A recent NBC News and People Magazine Poll reveals that 87 percent of teens aged 13 to 16 are not sexually active. Forty two percent of teens who are not sexually active attribute that choice to religious or moral beliefs. That makes me happy to know that. If you are ready for sex then you have to be ready for responsibility. They go hand in hand together. You have to know that the Creator of your life has given you the power of sex. You also have to know that He gave you sexual urges for you to control them and not for them to control you. What is so sad to me is that young men are encouraged in this society to freely engage in sexual activity but I don't know if you are aware of the significant risks to your life.

Sexually Transmitted Disease (STD's) Some facts for your consideration:

- Chlamydia is the most common STD, with more than 4 million cases each year.
- There are 200,000 to 500,000 new cases of genital herpes each year, but 31 million Americans are infected.
- Genital warts account for 1 million new infections each year, but at least 24 million people are infected.
- Gonorrhea infects at least 800,000 people each year.
- There are 120,000 cases of syphilis each year.
- Probably not surprising to most, Atlanta is one of the leading cities in rates of certain sexually transmitted diseases, according to a 1999 study conducted by the Centers for Disease Control and Prevention. The study showed that the state of Georgia, statistically, has one of the highest rates of gonorrhea and syphilis in the nation. According to the report, Atlanta is also on the list of top 20 cities for rates of both gonorrhea and syphilis.

There are now both men and women out here in America and in your community that know that they have the A.I.D.S. virus and are actively striving to infect as many people as possible with the disease. I want you to understand this. Let me say this again. Unfortunately you live in a world where people who know they have the A.I.D.S. virus are willingly going out to clubs and other places to share it with as many people as they can. The people who are doing this include males and females. I am not saying you need to have some blood work on any potential partner that may come your way but you never know what circles people are currently running in or used to run in. You need some kind of proof that your girlfriend's blood is clean. I know Usher sang that he wanted to make love in this club but you had better be mindful of the reality of what you just read. The wise men and women reminded me that our blood is our life.

I have met many young men who have two or three relationships that they are striving to maintain at one time. One young man called himself 'schooling me' and told me the way relationships go down out here nowadays. He said, **"First you get her name, then you get her number. Then you get some, get some, in the front seat of the hummer."** He went on to tell me, **"You have to have your main shorty. She is the one you take to Burger King and McDonalds. She's the one that you have unprotected sex with. Then you have to get you about three or four rips (other females) to just cut with (have sex with)."** So many young men are now caught up in having sex with any and every female that's willing to do **'a little sumethin, sumethin.'** Young men seem to love to callously share the names they have developed for these kinds of *'free for all'* kinds of females. Some females are now called:

Blockheads	**Hood Rats**
Pigeons	**The infamous B---- word**
Hoes	**Tricks**

I am always grateful for this kind of information. The other day I heard one of the worst names that I have ever heard a female ever be called. This young man told this other female in one of my classes that she was nothing but a **"rip". I asked him what did he mean by rip. He said to me that he called her a rip because to him all she was is a rip or slit in her body for him to have sex with and be out of there.** Now, think about that for a minute. You have to be mindful as a young man that every time you engage in sexual intercourse it is estimated that 50,000,000 sperm cells come out. Could you imagine having some female whom you thought of as and referred to as a rip, a blockhead, or some freak you just met at a club tell you that she was pregnant with your baby? **Three to five minutes of fun and folly could mean a lifetime of sadness and regret for you.** Imagine if she decided to keep the baby. What **would** she teach your child and even scarier to consider is what **could** she teach your child? For many years, females have been told to be mindful of the type of males they lay down with and produce children. I am cautioning you to be ever so careful as a male about the type of female you choose to be the mother of your seed.

A female is not a rip. The wise men and women have thoroughly taught me the true identity of the female so that I may share it with you. Read these words slowly and carefully. A young man that is striving to be 'a nobody' really doesn't **deserve** a female nor does he **need** a female. I encourage you to leave a female alone if you don't have anything going on in your life that you need her to help you with. Get your life in better shape before you 'holla' at her. A female is a serious creation of the Creator. You have much to learn about her. It's amazing how many males out here are so disrespectful of females and the females go for it. Many females willingly **accept** to be disrespected and many **expect** to be disrespected. As a male, where did you learn to treat females in the right way? Who taught you how to love, honor and respect females? Probably no one did. And that's sad. Because a female has the potential to be the greatest blessing that ever came into your life. She's certainly is not any of these low and filthy terms that many males so callously use to describe females. Unfortunately, I have been around plenty of females who now use those same filthy and degrading terms to describe themselves. Females have to learn their greatness just as you do. How can you be a prince and she not be a princess? How can you be on your way to becoming a king and she not be on her way to becoming a queen? *The wise men and women have taught me that it takes a good man to bring out the best in a female and it takes a good woman to bring out the best in a male.* A female is the only creature on the earth that can take a male's sperm into her womb and in nine months give him back the image and likeness of himself. That's powerful young brother. The Creator has already programmed her to be able to do this for you at a certain point in her development. The wise men and women have taught me that the only thing that you could equate the pain that a woman is going through while she is working to deliver the baby into the world for you is the pain of death itself. **So the female has to be willing to die to have your baby.** You may not have thought about it like that. I didn't either. Everyone has to really evaluate how we view females in our society. As males, we devalue females when we think of her as only being valuable for procreation and pleasure. Your generation has to see females as talented or gifted. You are not going anywhere as a male without the female. I don't care how great you become as a young man, it will take some female somewhere on this planet to bring you to the unknown heights that you aspire to. When you join successfully with the female then you both will be sharers in the development of this society, this nation and this civilization or you might choose to bring in a brand new one through her powerful womb.

I strive very hard to respect all females. I don't care how uncivilized a female may be acting, I just keep on displaying the fine wisdom the wise men and women have taught me. A female cannot resist a young man who has control of himself. A female cannot resist a young man that has control over his hands and his mouth. You don't need to cuss females. You don't need to be rough with a female. Females respond very well to a young man who's head is filled with knowledge, wisdom and understanding. You must not be an abusive young man and beat up females with your fists or with your mouth. I hate domestic violence. I despise the way young men and women are beating each other down all over America. **If you have to beat on a female then you don't need her.** No matter how uncivilized a female is the wise men and women taught me to never treat them in an indecent manner. You know platinum or gold has no consciousness and does not know its value. We place the value on them. Look at this society and the value it has placed on women. It's disgusting. The movies, the videos and the music that we constantly see and hear help to give males their worst ideas about females. Look at the videos and the movies that have come out over the last several years. What are they really promoting to you on HBO or Showtime or these other cable channels? What is their real agenda? How come no matter what the movie is about, they always seem to end up at the strip club? Because men in this society have not given or placed a proper value on the female then this is what causes females to devalue her self. The behavior of most of our grown women, young women and girls demonstrate the thinking of a devalued human being. And that's why she calls you a dog as a male and you quickly call her a female dog. If you really look at it we are getting further and further away from what it really means to be human beings. We are looking more and more like animals in heat as we try to relate to each other except we are a more worse off. A real dog can't be anything but a dog but what can you say for a human being that is acting like a dog. That's why I'm so grateful to the wise men and women for teaching me. I will forever be grateful. When you are taught better then your knowledge will force you to do better. What really helped me was when the wise men and women asked me to consider this point. **They said to me that if a female was able to take sperm into her womb and create a human life out worthless water then what could she do if she was impregnated with a man's ideas?** They went on to teach me that every female has two wombs. One at the top of their heads and the other womb I have just finished telling you about. The womb of the female's mind is fabulous. Most young men are terrified and afraid over the minds of females. This may be why they choose to use such cheap and disgraceful terms on her. Maybe they have to try to reduce her down to her other body parts because that may be the only way they can deal with her. You already know and may hang out with some guys who honestly believe that females are nothing to seriously consider. To those guys, a female is not a mind, a heart, or a wonderful spirit. She's a rip. She's a small rip or cut in the center of her body. Many of the songs that you might love on the radio today are attempting to reduce the stature of a female to nothing. Many songs make you think that the only value of a female is her ability to **'shake what her momma gave her'** or to **'shake that thang.'** In a recent song the artist Akon sings the hook:

"I see you windin n grindin up on that pole, I know u see me lookin' at you and you already know I wanna love you, you already know I wanna love you, you already know"

You already know that it the edited version of the song. Some of the newer songs seem intent on making the strip club the most appealing place a young man can go. The message of the new songs is reaching your age group in a most destructive way. How does a seventh grader handle the heavy messages that R. Kelly provides in part 118 of his adventures of being trapped in the closet? Travel with me into schoolhouses all over America and meet young girls in kindergarten whose life ambition is to be a stripper! Join me, and I promise you that we will meet first and second grade boys who will gleefully share that they are now in love with a stripper. Meet the fifth grade girl who has newfound popularity because her milkshake brings all the boys to the yard. She now invites all the boys in her class to **"check up on it."** Check up on what? **"Her lumps, her lovely lady lumps."** This is what I am now hearing in the schoolhouses that I go into.

Many guys claim to love their mother. They claim to love their sisters and other assorted female family members. I always ask them, **"Why is it okay for you to go out and mistreat someone else's daughter, sister or future mother and then be so adamant that no one had better do the same to your family?"** They never really have an answer for that one. The universe that we live in is constructed on a **'as you sew so you shall you also reap basis.'** Whatever you put out in the universe, good or bad, will be returned to you. Be careful about how you go out into this world and treat females. I repeat this to all of my male groups. There is no greater Creation in the existence of the universe than the female. She is the most magnificent of all of the Creator's creations and every female is actually worthy to be revered. In today's times so many young women are devoid of the true knowledge of themselves just like their male counterparts. The wise men and women have said to me that, **"Where there are no decent women, there will never be any decent men."** That tidbit of information from them is so true it's scary. One of the reasons that males are not decent in this society is that everywhere he looks females are exposed fully for his viewing pleasure. How can a normal young man function in a respectful fashion looking at a young woman's belly button, her feet and toes, her derriere, or 'padunk a dunk', or her breasts? Young women ought to at least give males a fighting chance and strive to cover up some of their finery! As long as females refuse to cover their finery then young men will continue to be the dogs that they helped to create because they appealed to the lowest part of the male. The wise men and women have shared with me that where there are no decent women, there will be no decent men.

Females are not the only valuable creations of the Creator but every male is as well. Your selection of the right female is critical to you and to the future of your family. You would be well advised to slow down to a complete stop if you are sexually active out here. The wise men and women told me to warn you that your generation is now leading in all new A.I.D.S.

cases. Your generation now has very high rates in many of the sexually transmitted disease categories. Do you already have a sexually transmitted disease for your personal collection? Do you want one? A female in her **right mind** is never too quick to want to lie down and have sex with some dude that she just met. Many men are now dealing with so many issues today because of their recklessness yesterday. Remember the words of the late, great prophet, Tupac Shakur. He said in one of his songs, **"I don't want it if it's that easy."**

One of the things that you want to gain is some skill in choosing a female that has a very good head on her shoulders. A smart female can really help you to become a real man one day in this world. Know this! Some female is going to have to absorb all of **your immaturity, your foolishness** and **your ignorance** out of you like a giant sponge. Until a female absorbs those things from you then you may never be anyone great. Some males are too selfish to allow a female to get close enough to them to do these things for him. It is true that the love of a female is intimidating for some males. Some young men intentionally sabotage the relationships with a female if she gets too close. But don't be afraid of her love young man. If she really loves you, all the negative things she finds out about you will be her little secret. This is why you love Alicia Keys when she sang the beautiful hook to her song, 'The Diary of Alicia Keys:

"I	won't	tell	your	secrets
Your	secrets	are	safe	with	me
I	will	keep	your	secrets
Just think of me as the pages in your diary"

Yes, young man, you really do need to re-evaluate your thinking concerning the female population. You need her and she needs you. **You will not be able to find in another male what the female has been made by nature from our Creator to offer to you.** You need to really invest some time into a female to see if she is worthy to be the mother of your future. What do I mean? Look at the word father. The idea behind producing children is that one day this child will be able to go further than what you did in the world. A father should want his children to go further than he goes. If you have no relationship with the baby's mother whatsoever then you may not stick around long enough to see what that child eventually becomes in life. It's very easy to rack up 3 or 4 children that you have fathered out of wedlock in a relatively short amount of years by 3 or 4 different girls or women. *I recently heard about a young man that was 24 years old who had already*

fathered 10 children in the world. Do you really want your baby mother to have 4 children by 4 different baby daddies before you get with her? This is the life of a mack, a pimp or a hustler. They may have enough money flowing through their hands to deal with something like that but will you? Right now you are probably broke and all you have to take care of is yourself. How are you realistically going to tell me that you want your baby to come and live with you? I mean it's nice to want a baby but are you really ready for a child in your life? Some mothers encourage their sons in these kinds of endeavors by telling him they want a grandbaby. I always wonder if she is really ready to become a grandmother. So the young man goes out and makes a baby in order for her to be a grandmother. But he wasn't interested in being a father. He was just trying to satisfy his mommy's wishes.

Did you know that it's more to being a father than you think? Trust me. I have been blessed to father six children. Yes, let that sink in. All six of my children are through my beautiful wife, Cecelia. All of them are blessed to have the same mother and father. All of them live with my wife and me as well. We didn't have any children until **after** we were married. We tried to do it right. I knew when I met her that she was the one for me. I don't know how I knew that back then but I have always loved her. I can honestly tell young men this, what you call love now at 14, 15, 16, 17, 18, and 19 years of age will be nothing compared to your understanding of love when you turn 30, 40 and 50 years old. I encourage you to take your time with all females and to settle on a good choice. Sex before marriage is going to always cloud your mind and interfere with your ability to make a good decision. Don't make the mistake and think that sex is all that a female is looking for from you. If you think you have found the 'tender roni' that is right for you before you make it official I really recommend the process of courtship to you. Courtship is your opportunity to explore one another is a non-sexual way. The purpose of courtship will help you and your potential future spouse to determine your readiness for marriage.

Do you have any idea how many young and old men are struggling to pay child support today? How many men are behind bars due to not paying child support? When you cannot support the children that you help to conceive then many times the baby's mother must get on welfare and seek other support services from the city government where she lives. Every dollar that they give her in aid begins to get tied to your name as the identified father. Even when a father goes to jail for not paying his child support money he is still held responsible for all the new aid that the young lady is receiving for the care of the baby. The point that I'm making to you as a young man is that your poor outlook on the female gender could wreak complete havoc in your life. Tina Turner expressed powerful lyrics in her ground breaking song, **"What's love got to do with it?"** She sang in the hook to that song, **"Oh what's love got to do, got to do with it. What's love but a second hand emotion? What's love got to do, got to do with it. Who needs a heart when a heart can be broken?"** This song was applicable to my generation but is extremely applicable to your generation. Where is the love? There are millions of children in America that were conceived by two people who had no love or any real feeling for each other, other than 100% lust. Society and the current laws on the books most definitely favor the female. You can be a gigolo if you want to and have babies all over the place but you still have to pay the cost to be the boss. Child Support can and will eat up your money. It's better to get married and do it the right way. Try to have all of your children by one woman. I wouldn't recommend having a son over here and a daughter over there. I remember a song that they used to play on the radio by the great **"Temptations"** when I was coming up. The song was entitled, **"Papa was a rolling stone."** The hook on the lyrics went:

      "Papa was a rolling stone, wherever he laid his hat was his home / And when he died, All he left us was alone"

This song always saddens me when I hear it because that song was reality for too many young men when I was growing up. It is an even greater reality among this generation of young men.

What are the types of learning styles?

Visual Learners:

Learn through seeing. These learners need to see the teacher's body language and facial expression to fully understand the content of a lesson. They tend to prefer sitting at the front of the classroom to avoid visual obstructions (e.g. people's heads). They may think in pictures and learn best from visual displays including: diagrams, illustrated text-books, overhead transparencies, videos, flipcharts and hand-outs. During a lecture or classroom discussion, visual learners often prefer to take detailed notes to absorb the information.

Auditory Learners:

Learn through listening. They learn best through verbal lectures, discussions, talking things through and listening to what others have to say. Auditory learners interpret the underlying meanings of speech through listening to tone of voice, pitch, speed and other nuances. Written information may have little meaning until it is heard. These learners often benefit from reading text aloud and using a tape recorder.

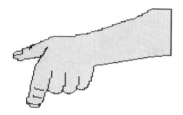

Tactile/Kinesthetic Learners:

Learn through, moving, doing and touching. Tactile/Kinesthetic persons learn best through a hands-on approach, actively exploring the physical world around them. They may find it hard to sit still for long periods and may become distracted by their need for activity and exploration.

Which way do you learn best?

Chapter Four – Where are you going?

Whether you want to admit this or not, time is moving. I'm sure that you can remember when you were just a little boy going to school for your very first time. A few days later, you looked up and found that you were in middle school. A few days later you were in 11th grade in high school. Time doesn't wait on any of us. If you don't sit down and develop a plan of personal action for your life you will be sorry. If you don't develop a plan for your life, someone else will. They will come right up to you and ask you, **"What are you doing?"** And then if you respond, **"I ain't doing nothing"**, then he'll give you his agenda. Even if it's a bad agenda you can't refuse it because you ain't doing nothing no way! And this is why so many young men fill the juvenile detention centers and jails in America. In some respects, adults have failed to teach you how to think and to plan for your own good and benefit. Many young men are caught up in having fun and a good time. And there is nothing wrong with having fun and a good time. Just remember that along the way at a certain time you will have to sit down and plan something for tomorrow. Don't you want to be better off tomorrow than what you may be today? The wise men and women sent me to tell you that the future belongs to those who prepare for it today. There is a saying that he who fails to plan, plans to fail. Do you have a plan to fail? Or will you develop a plan to succeed? Do you need some help in order to do that? *Planning is simply thinking in advance of what needs to be done tomorrow. What will need to get done tomorrow that you can at least start on today?* Tomorrow you will need to have legal money coming in. So today you need to learn what skills employers are forecasting will be needed for the jobs of tomorrow. You might want to be an entrepreneur. Whatever business you decide to get involved with should be legal. Don't think small. Think big! Think about owning a chain of whatever business you choose. Think about how you are going to put one in all fifty states. See yourself legally operating your company and giving thousands of people jobs because of your brilliance. You know it's possible for a young man of your caliber. Once you have a personal plan of action together for your life then learning new things will become enjoyable for you because you will have something to apply what you are learning to. That's one of the reasons that some young men don't like learning. They have nothing going on to apply the knowledge to. If you don't develop a personal plan of action for your life then you may end up looking for yet another program or group to be a part of. You may also end up following someone else's plan. That happens more than you know.

Once you have been inspired by someone and something and you have a personal plan of action together for your life, then you can apply what you have just learned immediately to help you achieve your plans. You can try and put that information to good use for yourself. If you don't use that new information quickly, then you may lose your inspiration and then be back in the same situation that you were in a week, a month or a year ago.

Many times I have asked young men what do they need in life to help them to be successful. Some say, **"I don't need anything or anybody."** The wise men and women have sent me to inform you that this simply is not the case. They said that was completely the wrong attitude for anybody to adopt in today's times. Everything that you do in life will be done because someone helped you to do it and to accomplish it. You will never be able to say, **"I did it all by myself."** How can you say that you don't need anything? Don't you need to continue living? Do you really recognize that you are alive and that this is the only moment that you will ever have to be here on the planet? Do you believe that you have not come to this planet by accident? Do you believe that there is a reason that you are here? The wise men and women have sent me to tell you that there is nothing in the universe in which we live that is here without an aim or a purpose. Every atom serves a purpose; every insect and every animal serves a purpose. The sun, the moon and every star serve a purpose. Every planet in our solar system serves a purpose. There is no such thing as something or somebody coming into existence and no purpose or function was assigned to its life. Think about that. That's why you should never take from another human being what you could never give, like the gift of life. That is another need that young men have. Young men have a need to solve the problems that naturally come up with other young people in a more peaceful fashion. You need to learn how to forgive. As you get older your first reaction is not supposed to be, **"I am going to shoot that so and so"**.

I recently heard about a young man that was beat up in a fair fight. He came home to his mother and explained to her what had happened. She gave him a loaded weapon and told him to go handle his business. He did. He shot and killed the young man that had beaten him in a fair fight. What is wrong with our young men today? **When did you get the idea in your heart and mind that you were not allowed to lose a fair fight to another young person?** Who has told you that you must shoot or stab or shank the person that beat you? Many times it is adults in general and we your parents who are peddling our ignorance to you. Parents today are some of the greatest conduits of ignorance to their children. Many parents try to relive their own twisted lives through the life of their sons and daughters. Whatever he couldn't do or she failed at when they were younger they sometimes encourage their son or daughter to do. One of the conscious rappers wisely said, **"Ignorance is at an all time high"**. So because this mother told her son to go handle his business he is now in jail charged with 1st degree murder and the mother is also behind bars charged with 2nd degree murder. You can't listen to the advice of everybody. You have to know who has good information to share and who doesn't. Everybody in your life is here to teach you a lesson. Some lessons are to teach you how to do something and some lessons are to teach you how not to do something. You have to learn how to identify what lesson this person is in your life to teach you. The wise men and women have sent me to tell you that you learn to carry something heavier on your shoulder than a chip or a grudge. Many young men have so much outer conflict with others because they have so much inner conflict within themselves. The more effectively you address your inner conflicts you will find that the outer conflicts will become completely unnecessary. It's not that you won't have problems or beefs with others. It's just that you will learn to handle them so much better.

We are still talking about where you are going. The way you feel today is not how you are going to feel tomorrow. The way you see things today will not be the way that you will see them tomorrow. I can personally guarantee that. And that is a blessing. You are moving towards manhood. I know the circumstances that brought you here to this earth may not have been the best circumstances. But if you take a little time to study history, you would find you are not the first to come to this earth through unfortunate circumstances. And that's a point to remember whenever life is not going the way you want it to go. It's important to know that the earth didn't just start rotating on its axis, spinning at the terrific speed of 1,037 1/3 miles per hour when you showed up. It's important to remember that the earth has been spinning for trillions of years and has many more to go before she will stop. You aren't the first person to have a problem or a beef with something or somebody. You have to learn patience as a young man. You have to be patient with yourself and with others. Somebody has had problems before you. I'm willing to bet that someone on the earth has your problem right now or has had your problem at some point. The question for you should always be, "How can I solve this problem". A young man has to always be thinking in terms of a solution to problems. Problems are a natural part of life. Therefore, you should look forward to solving problems. One of the ways that you can learn some different strategies to solving problems is to read more. Do you notice I keep coming back to reading more? The wise men and women told me to tell you this: **"Everything that you want to know is in a book somewhere."** They used to have a saying that if you wanted to hide something from a young man, put it in a book. That's the one place they would never think of looking. I am hurt to find out that so many young men don't know how to read and don't like to read. Many young men cover this fact up by trying to be a well-dressed dummy. They have on the latest clothes and the latest fashions but they cannot read. Ignorance is not funny. Being ignorant causes a horrible chain reaction. The less you read, the less you cultivate your mind, your heart and your spirit. The less you read the **more** uncivilized you will become. This lack of civility will be reflected in your behavior, in your language, in your style of dress and in the way you act at home and in public. Then you find that people who are working on their civility will not desire to be around you. Then you may start acting like a savage. The wise men and women have said, **"A savage is a person that has lost the knowledge of self and is living a beast life."** Many of our young men look like they have crawled out of some cave somewhere. Their hair is all over the place. Their pants are hanging as low as they can hang. And it's not necessarily your fault. Too many grown men and women in your communities are trying to be just like you. Nowadays you can catch a 79 year old man riding on dubs, blasting Lil Jon talking about, **"Snap your fingers, do your step. You can do it all by yo self, let me see you do it."** So many of our elders haven't got their own personal act together and yet want to tell you as a young person to do as they say and not as they do. But the wise men and women sent me here to tell you that the best way to change the behavior of another human being is to be that human beings example.

It is extraordinarily important that you know where you want to go in your life. An overwhelming majority of young men only have a vague idea of why they are alive or where they are headed. You have to open your eyes. Can you answer with clarity, why you get up in the morning? Have you ever considered why you even go to school or why you have to do this and why do you have to do that? You have to think about these things now. What is your reason for being in the world? What have you come here to do? What have you come here to say to the world? What message does this world really need right now? What have you come to teach this world? What have you come to learn from this world? What is your mission in life? What is your purpose? **How will the earth be better because you came this way? These are serious things to think about. What will your contribution be to the onward march of civilization?** Doesn't this world have enough murderers, killers, rapists, robbers, gangsters, pimps, pushers, drug dealers and users in it? Why would you want to aspire to be like that? How would becoming that bring honor and respect to your blessed mother? Too many young men when confronted with these simple questions don't have a clue. Many young men don't even have the desire to lead a life of consequence among their peers. There is so much pressure to conform in the lives of young men today and be just like everyone else. It is so refreshing for me to meet young men who have their own mind and have opinions on the pressing issues of our day.

You have to be very careful about what you choose to focus on in such an hour as this. You can choose to focus on whatever you want to. Many young men choose to focus on what's wrong in their lives instead of what is going right. You see you have to focus on what you are becoming versus what you are right now. You have to focus on what you want. Please do not focus on what you don't want. It is important that you know that you will not attract what you want, but that which you are. That is why I keep emphasizing the question, **"Who are you?"** Because you can only attract what you are. If all your friends are trifling, then you have to ask the question, **"Why do I keep attracting trifling people."** If all your friends are idiots, then you have to ask the question, **"Why do I attract idiots?"** The attraction may be something right inside of you. You have to be careful about following your friend's advice. Remember their knowledge is a mixture of facts, their imaginations, partly understood personal experiences, guesses, and of course false information. Thus, their knowledge is defective. Nor does their mental grasp comprehend all of the ultimate truths because they haven't even learned them yet.

Maybe you spend too much time looking at others. Maybe you have become skilled in the art of finding out what's wrong with somebody else and can't seem to identify what's wrong with you. The only reason we look outward is to reflect back in. Whenever you don't like another person's actions, it may be because you have seen that same kind of quality in yourself. And if you haven't corrected it in yourself, then you don't have the power to correct it in anyone else because you can't be that person's example.

In the course of the next few years, you will discover many aspects about yourself that you may not like. And coincidentally, it may be some of the same things that others have shared with you. The way it works is very interesting. I don't care how much your mother, your father, your sisters, your brothers, your friends, teachers, and others tell you about your shortcomings; it is not until you take notice of it, that you can change it. Sometimes our faults are shared with us privately where we can correct the problem and move on with our lives. But at that point, if we don't do anything about it, then it may be found out by a few more people and then if we still don't do anything about it soon everyone will know we have this problem.

So many young men choose to get involved in the drug game. One of the worst people in the world is the young man who is self deluded. Many young men think they're slick, smooth, stealthy, and have the ability to operate below the radar. They constantly reference dreams of being the new 'Scar face' in their communities. Some brag that they have watched that film twenty or thirty times. Do you really think that no one knows who you are? Do you really think that the police department, the sheriff's department, the county police and the state police do not know every square inch of the county that they are presiding over? The drug business is a huge business in this country. A trillion dollars a year are spent on drugs. The big boys at the top never touch drugs or have it on their person at any time. It's the little fellow that wants to make a big name for himself, wants to have a fat knot of money, and thinks he will never get caught. Isn't he surprised when the drug bust goes down at 3:42am in the morning when he was fast asleep and he's carted off to jail in his yellow Sponge Bob boxer shorts? Maybe as you read this, you have the dream of being the next little flip. Maybe you have it in your mind that you are going to get in the game for a few months and keep flipping some product until you can get up a respectable amount of dough up. Many young men are in jail today that thought the same way. Maybe you grew up a little screw – up and got introduced to the game and then you blew up. Maybe you haven't fully thought about the consequences yet. Some young men don't care about the consequences. They love it. They are following everything the rap music suggests. The one thing I never hear the music talk about too much are the consequences. Do you really want to devote five, ten or twenty years of your life to a small jail cell that you have to be in 23 hours a day? Is your freedom really worth that?

Where are you going with a drug problem? If you don't know it yet, if you are smoking weed, you have a drug problem. If you are into that **ecstasy** or other kinds of **purple pills**, that **'kush'**, that **'AK47'**, that **'blueberry'**, that **'Northern lights'** or that **'alpine swiss'** right now as a young man then what will you be using in the future? I meet so many young men who get high before they get to school. And they are leaning off of that promethazine all the way through school. I had a friend that stayed high all of the time. He affectionately called his weed habit, **"His friend."** He told me that smoking was the first thing he did in the morning, in the afternoon and at the end of the day. He told me that before he got with his girl he smoked because he believed that being high somehow enhanced his experiences with his girl. All kinds of ignorance are attached to smoking weed. I spoke with this same person a few months ago and he let me know that he had been diagnosed with lung cancer. It's to every young man's advantage to take this check up from the neck up now before your drug abuse or alcohol abuse catches up with you. We all have something in our lives that we need to get under control. After all, this is our very life that we are talking about.

Analyze your own Appearance and Speech

The ancients all said "Know Thyself." In line with this, try to objectively find out what sort of impression you make on others. Actually, it's all a matter of degree... no one's appearance is really perfect and no one's is really terrible. How much should you improve?

Study the Impression Others Make

Don't copy others, but observe them to discover how their appearance affects other people... things such as size, mannerisms, and voice. Notice how important these are to business and social acceptance.

Get Others to Describe the Impression You Make

This technique can be painful, but some people feel it helps. Unfortunately, "We see ourselves differently from the way others see us." A frank, confidential discussion with a respected friend or associate might uncover a few offensive habits that can be corrected.

Set up a Grooming Schedule

Perhaps you need to set up a personal schedule to guarantee enough time for: weekly haircuts, a good shave, proper nail care, pressed and cleaned suits, daily shoe shine, necktie changes, etc. These things don't just happen, they have to be planned.

Use more Precise Words

John Wannamaker kept a daily list of new words that he looked up in a dictionary every night. He claimed that checking these words was as much fun as reading a mystery novel. A good vocabulary is a strong asset to anyone.

Move your Lips when Speaking

This improves enunciation. Voice training can help personal leadership. Find out whether your voice helps or hurt the impression you make.

Stress Key Phrases When Talking

Stressing key phrases helps you win attention. Some Ministers and Pastors have mastered this technique. Learn to give emphasis once in a while by making your voice softer. It causes listeners to exert themselves to hear you. It's called the **"whisper technique."**

Try Raising Your Voice on the Last Words

When you raise your voice on the last words (just before you finish speaking), it has a powerful effect on listeners. There are many other methods of making conversations more dynamic, and therefore, more effective.

Talk in Phrases --- With Brief Pauses

If you try --- talking in phrases --- as this shows --- with a little pause --- after each phrase--- it makes it easier--- for others to listen---and for you to organize---what you have to say.

Try Walking Better

Your walk expresses some of your personality. It can show you to be confident or timid, enthusiastic or lazy, careless or lazy, careless or exact. How do you think a stranger would judge you by your walk?

How well are you organized? Assessing where you are in Managing Your Time: "...Planning is determining in advance what is to be done in the future...

- Do you take the time that is necessary to plan for work or your life in general?
Yes _____ **No** _____
- Do you have a schedule book, a PDA or a planner that you actually use?
Yes _____ **No** _____
- Are you constantly interrupted during the day and find it hard to make time to complete the work projects you are working on... **Yes** _____ **No** _____
- I have a personal desk at my house for my important business
Yes _____ **No** _____
- *My* desk and work area is disorganized. It is full of clutter and takes me a while to find things. **Yes** _____ **No** _____
- I find it hard to say "NO" to requests for my time during the day.
Yes _____ **No** _____
- I use scraps of paper, desk pads and sticky notes (or my memory) to remember things. **Yes** _____ **No** _____
- I know I should make more quality time for "myself" in life, but justify it by telling myself I don't have enough time (and that one day I will have more time).
Yes _____ **No** _____
- I frequently wake up late and find myself rushing at break neck speed to be on time. **Yes** _____ **No** _____
- In the past month I have completely forgotten, or been significantly late to an appointment, meeting or important activity or event at work. **Yes** _____ **No** _____
- I find work repetitive and boring. **Yes** _____ **No** _____
- I drink more than 4 cans of soda or coffee at home or work a week.
Yes _____ **No** _____
- I start getting depressed on Sunday nights as I begin to think about going back to work or to some program. **Yes** _____ **No** _____
- I procrastinate or postpone decisions. My mind wanders off-track when I'm about to work on something. **Yes** _____ **No** _____
- I ask for help for some things which I could handle in less time by myself.
Yes _____ **No** _____
- I can't seem to decide on what to do next when I do get around to doing some work at home. **Yes** _____ **No** _____
- I go to work without an adequate personal goal or priorities for the days work. **Yes** _____ **No** _____

Chapter Five – How are you going to get there?

This is the concluding chapter of this book. It is the last question I want you to really think about. How are you going to get there? Is what I have shared with you through this book possible or impossible for you to even conceive? I'll bet you didn't realize that there is so much work for you to do on yourself. If you commit to yourself that you are going to do a little of the work I've identified to you that has to be done then you'll get there. If you throw this book aside and other insightful materials aside then you may continue to go the way of millions of our young men out here. I am just trying to prevent young men from ever saying that nobody ever told them how to be a great man. I am trying to prevent you from pointing your finger at somebody and saying it's all your fault! I am hoping that this book is helping you to focus on your great destiny that is right in front of you. So here is the final wrap up for you that will set you on the road to success.

The art of asking questions: One of the smartest things you can ever do as a young man is to learn how to ask the right questions. **You do this by diligently** studying communication techniques  from people who are pretty good at it. Smart, intelligent, wise young men constantly employ questions while communicating with others. They know that questions are a valuable communication technique. Asking questions helps you to avoid false assumptions. You have probably been in a situation where someone has falsely assumed your thoughts or actions. False assumptions are nearly always bad, even if a good thing is assumed, therefore adding unnecessary stress to you as a young man. Asking questions helps you to understand a person's thoughts, position, or condition. By asking a question or two you may be able to determine another person's mental or emotional state or condition. Questions are valuable in answering questions. Answering a question with a question is valuable by engaging the questioner in the response causing him to logically think through the response. Think back to most of the teachers you really liked at school. Most of them were people who made you think. Good teachers always employ questions in their teachings. How many Churches have you gone into where you witnessed the Pastor or Minister asking what is called rhetorical questions? These kinds of questions are asked in order to keep an audience or a person engaged and helps them to see your point when your speaking. Asking questions is the first rule of effective interpersonal communication.

When are questions effective in communication? When in doubt, ask a question. To understand someone, ask a question. When defending your position, ask a question. When answering a question, ask a question. When teaching somebody, ask a question. In general, start questions with **"how,"** **"what,"** **"where,"** **"why"** or **"when."** Think that's obvious? When you ask a question, there's nothing more important than generating a true and honest curiosity about the answer. That's why open-ended questions are best for most situations that will come up in your life. Try to avoid yes / no questions because they're usually a dead end. **In contrast, open-ended questions:** invite opinions, thoughts and feelings; encourages participation; establishes rapport with your partner; stimulates discussion; and maintains balance between you and your partner. I recommend that you do a little more research on these types of questions: **Factual questions, Interpretive questions**, and **Evaluative questions**.

The power of listening: Do you know what the hardest lesson I ever learned in my life was? It was to listen. To get to where you want to go you are going to have to listen to somebody. Listen with everything you got. The wise men and women have taught me that listening is hard work. It requires your complete concentration. You need to use not only your ears, but also your eyes to listen. Many times you can learn more by what the other person doesn't say than by what he does say. You should watch the changing tone and volume of his / her voice. Sometimes you'll find a meaning that is in direct contrast to his / her spoken words. Watch the facial expressions, their mannerisms, their gestures, their movements of their eyes and their overall body language. I had to realize that although I had learned and I knew a little something, I didn't know nearly enough about what life was all about. You don't either. You have a long, long way to go. So many young men don't listen to anyone.

Find a strong man to be like: Many young men have had to raise themselves. I hope that you have had the benefit of a good mother or father or grandparents in your life to do the best they could with you. Many young men still feel like there is something missing in their lives. By the time that most young men start turning twelve and thirteen years old something started to happen within them. They started to need a man in their lives. Hold on. I'm not trying to say you are gay or something. But you need a man in your life. For what? I've already shared with you that it takes a man to show you how to be a man. **How can you know except you have a teacher? How can that teacher come except he be sent?** The same is true for a young woman.

It takes a real woman to show a young woman how to be a real woman. Young women need the presence of a strong male image in their lives as well. It helps to slow down the puberty process. A young woman doesn't have to grow up so fast when a strong male image or a father figure is present in the house. A father should protect his daughters and not hit on them or abuse them or try to get with them in a sexual manner. So many young women that I work with have never known the love of a father. I have read that it is estimated that 70% of young women have been abused. Young men certainly need a strong male image in their lives. You don't go to the jungle and find a pussy cat trying to rear a lion. A few years ago I was watching a movie called the Lion King. If little Simba had never seen his father Mufassa roar, then how would he know what a roar sounded like? Many of our young men have never had a real man in their lives to model what a real man looks like and acts like. You would be hard pressed to go throughout some communities and find men who desire to be real men in today's time.

Accept good guidance and give good guidance: If you were to accept the wisdom and council of the wise men and women it would help you to get where you are going. Just look at the principles that I have espoused to you from them. **You might be wondering who are these wise men and women anyway.** The wise men and women is every adult that has ever tried to guide you in a positive direction. Members of your family, your teachers, your elders, your church members are also a part of this group. **As a young man you have to understand that you are surrounded by knowledge, wisdom and understanding.** You don't have to figure it all out yourself. You could be a mental giant in the world instead of a mental midget. You could choose to major in great things versus majoring in minor things.

You have to develop common sense. Common sense has never been that common. It is often a very lonely road that you will walk when you learn how to think for yourself and do for yourself. One of the saddest realities I had to confront is that you can't make anybody do anything. You can tell your friends what you believe is the right way for them to go but in the end they have to choose that road for themselves. You cannot make them see what you see. People are stubborn and generally hate good advice. Take all of your advice and common sense and apply it to your own life. It is only when you are able to be an example of the advice that you seek to give that people may listen to you. The moment you give somebody advice they are going to start looking at you and judging you to see whether you have got your act together. So get your act together before you try to worry so much about everyone else.

Finish what you start: You have probably been permitted to start things and never finish them. Young men are sometimes so enthusiastic at the beginning of things they start. But the wise men and women sent me to tell you that you must not just be a great starter, you must also be a great finisher. Develop the habit that whatever you do in your life, you will try with all your heart to do well. Whatever you have devoted yourself to, devote yourself to complete. I know it's altogether too common to start on something, and then never quite finish it. What good is starting something, if you don't finish it?

Understand the mentality of some young men: Some young men can be great time wasters. Some young men hate to see another young man be productive and be about their business. That's why the wise men and women have said that you must always know where **you** are going at all times. Please understand that while you are young you shouldn't get wrapped up in any one particular group of friends. Try to forge friendships with as many people as possible. Everything that you are going to attempt to get done will have to be done through other people. You have to learn people. People are different. You may think you know how people are but I believe that there is so much more for you to learn. When young men get caught up in only one group of friends then that young man starts to lose his focus. Instead of who am I, where am I going, how am I going to get there and who is going to help me it becomes who are we, where are we going, how are we going to get there and who is going to help us. In every group that I have been apart of, someone had to lead and someone had to follow. You will always know the leader in a group because when they move, the others move. This is a natural principle. Sometimes young men will challenge each other for the leadership of the group. Sometimes this will result in a fight or a contest of wills to see who will lead. Many times the leader of the group may just have physical strength and prowess. Many times they may just have the biggest mouth. But this can be dangerous to everyone who is part of the group because sometimes that person can be out of control. Ask yourself these questions. **Am I the leader in the groups that I am involved with? If I am the leader then where am I taking the people to? Where am I guiding them?** The wise men and women have taught me a lot about leadership. They have said that leadership is nothing to play with. It is an awesome responsibility to have people to look to you for leadership. When they do you need to be sure where you are going. When people are following you they are depending on you to see what's in front of them because they are behind you and following you. If the blind lead the blind then both will fall into the ditch. **Are you a follower in the groups that you are involved with?** You still need some idea where the one or the ones you are following are leading you. Everyone will lead someone in their lifetime and everyone at some point has to follow. One thing to remember is the kind of leader you are going to be will be determined by the kind of follower you are. If you cannot follow then you will never be able to lead. **Where can the person or the people you are following take you? Are you on the right team? Are you on a winning team? Is your/their leadership headed down the right road?**

      Be mindful: Never let others know how much you really have. I have already shared with you that people can be great time wasters. People can also be great users. Never let people borrow things from you unless you are sure that you don't want it back anymore. Don't flaunt jewelry or money in front of people. Everyone doesn't appreciate how well you may be doing and many robberies turn out to be inside jobs. Keep other young men away from your personal space as much as possible. Keep them out of your room and be mindful of them when they are in your house. Set rules with your friends and limitations. Always get your own stuff. Never borrow clothes or money from your friends. People can become horrible when you owe them something. Get your own transportation. This is critical. Make sure your car is in your name. Never allow more than one young man into your car at a time. Be mindful of the way that you are dressed whenever you are out in public. Be mindful of the way that your friends are dressed. You do not want to bring unnecessary attention to yourselves do you? You have to watch how your friends act in public. Be mindful of their mindset. Are your friends crazy? Are they on drugs? Do they have drugs on them right now? Be mindful of the way they smell. Are they drunk? Are they drinking right now? I do not hang with anyone who has the philosophy that they are **'down for whatever.'** Whatever is too big of a word. Be an honorable son. Always let your parents know where you are and with whom you are. These are dangerous times. It is different from when I grew up. I could make a mistake in the past and live to tell about it. In today's times one mistake could cost you your life. I share these things with you so you may avoid the pitfalls that so many young men fall into. Never let your friends stop you from being about your personal agenda or plans. Never be afraid to be by yourself. You don't need your friends to agree with you when you are trying to do the right thing for your life. I try my best to have a destination in mind whenever I get into my car. I try to know where I am going to, who am I going to see, why I am going in the first place and what I will do once I am blessed to get there. Other than that I don't get in my car. **I have learned that part of why we**

sometimes end up in the wrong place at the wrong time is because we didn't have a right place to be. You have to choose to be in the right place at the right time. If you've got a plan, and systematically keep to that plan, returning to it after each interruption, you've got less chance of being derailed. It's the finishing that matters here. Finishing a job is the difference between a man and a male and between a girl and a woman. Throw yourself into a job. See it to a satisfactory conclusion, and then move on to a new challenge to conquer.

'Hatin': I'm sure that you know that some young men have such terrible attitudes about everything. They feel that life owes them something. And maybe you don't realize it, but life is doing it's part. Life is trying to give you an education. I have noticed that some young men constantly use this term called hating. They say, this one is **'hating on me'** or **'that one is hating on me'**. One of the rappers even has a song called, "Hi Hater". I understand this term to mean that perhaps somebody is envious or jealous of you. In some instances that may be true but everybody is 'not hating' on you. You would be surprised at how little time people actually spend thinking about *you*.

You did ask to come here: I know what some of you say. You say well, **"I didn't ask to come here!"** You are not being truthful and I think I can prove that you did want to be here. You have to use your brain to think with me though. Have you ever studied the way you came into existence? It is evident by your existence that your father and your mother did an act to conceive you. You are certainly the proof that somebody did something. As I referenced to you earlier, the scientists say that approximately 50 million sperm entered into the womb of your mother. Each of those sperm had a job to do which was to get to the egg of the female. Now none of those million to a billion sperm had arms, legs or a body or a brain to utilize. The sperm only had a head and a tail. There was no light in the womb of your mother. The darkest place in the universe is the womb of the female! The sperm had to travel upwards against the flow of gravity in complete and total darkness to get to the egg of the female. Think about this. Can you imagine what the competition was like in there? A million to a billion sperm cells trying to get to one egg. And you represent the one that made it! You won against a million to a billion to one odds and you prevailed! How in the world can you ever again say that you didn't ask to come here? How can you ever again accept some cheap term like 'pimp' or 'thug' to define you?

Stay away from crime and violence: I have done my very best to convince you through this book to stay away from the death style of crime and violence. Listed below are some statistics that you will need to know about what's currently happening with black men who are already out here. The Black Report compiled these statistics. Their report was called, **"The Silent Genocide - Facts about the Deepening Plight of Black Men in America"** Take this knowledge for what it's worth!

In Education/Family
• Only 45% of Black men graduate from high school in the United States.
• Just 22 % of Black males who began at a four-year college graduated within six years.
• 69% of Black children in America cannot read at grade level in the 4th grade, compared with 29% among White children.
• 7% of Black 8th-graders perform math at grade level.
• 32% of all suspended students are Black. Black students (mostly Black males) are twice as likely as Whites to be suspended or expelled.
• 67% of Black children are born out of wedlock.

In Employment/Economics
• At comparable educational levels, Black men earn 67% of what White men make.
• White males with a high-school diploma are just as likely to have a job and tend to earn just as much as Black males with college degrees.
• Blacks make up only 3.2% of lawyers, 3% of doctors, and less than 1% of architects in America. Many of these are Black women.
• 53% of Black men aged 25-34 are either unemployed or earn too little to lift a family of four from poverty.
• Light-skinned Blacks have a 50% better chance of getting a job than dark-skinned Blacks.
• While constituting roughly 12% of the total population, Black America represents nearly 30% of America's poor.
• 45% of Black children live below the poverty line, compared with 16% of White children.
• The net worth of a Black family in America is $6,100 versus $67,000 for a White family.
• In New York City in 2003 only 51.8% of Black men ages 16 to 64 were employed vs. 75.7% for White men and 65.7% for Latino men.
• White men with prison records receive far more offers for entry-level jobs in New York City than black men with identical records, and are offered jobs just as often - if not more so - than black men who have never been arrested.

In Incarceration/Crime:

• In 2001, the chances of going to prison were highest among Black males (32.2%) and Hispanic males (17.2%) and lowest among White males (5.9%).

• Blacks account for only 12% of the U.S. population, but 44 % of all prisoners in the United States are Black.

• Blacks, who comprise only 12% of the population and account for about 13% of drug users, constitute 35% of all arrests for drug possession, 55% of all convictions on those charges, and 74% of all those sentenced to prison for possession.

• In at least fifteen states, Black men were sent to prison on drug charges at rates ranging from twenty to fifty-seven times those of White men.

• In 1986, before mandatory minimums for crack offenses became effective, the average federal drug offense sentence for Blacks was 11% higher than for Whites. Four years later following the implementation of harsher drug sentencing laws, the average federal drug offense sentence was 49% higher for Blacks.

• 1,172 Black children and teenagers in the United States died from gunfire in 2003.

• A young Black male in America is more likely to die from gunfire than was any soldier in Vietnam.

• The Justice Department estimates that one out of every 21 Black men can expect to be murdered, a death rate double that of U. S. soldiers in World War II.

• 1.46 million Black men out of a total voting population of 10.4 million have lost their right to vote due to felony convictions.

Rep your city, put on for your city: Your respect for a person or thing cannot be greater than your knowledge of that particular person or thing. If a young person has little knowledge of something then they generally will have just as little respect for it. However, when you have a good bit of information of something you will generally respect it better and have a better attitude towards it. As a young man you have to choose to have a better attitude about wanting to know more about the city that you currently live in. The city that you are from is helping to birth you into the world. If you don't know anything about the city then just go to your local chamber of commerce in the city or look for your city on the internet. It's hard to respect the state where you are blessed to be born in if you don't first respect the city. How then will you have respect for the other areas of the country? Why would you have a desire to go out into the world and see what you don't have any information about? You can gain plenty of information about the rest of America whether it's the South, the East Coast, the Midwest, the Southwest and the West Coast. You don't have to stop there either. One of the reasons you may be irritable is because you haven't gone anywhere or seen anything in a while. The wise men and women have taught me that, **"Evil thoughts often come from idleness."**

You should want to know and see the seven continents of our Planet. You can want to know and see the whole of North America, South America, Europe, Antarctica, Asia, Australia, and Africa in your lifetime. You should want to see the Four Oceans of the earth. You should want to see The Arctic Ocean, the Atlantic Ocean, the Indian Ocean and the Pacific Ocean. The earth that you live on is **196,940,000 square miles**. The land covers **57,255,000 square miles** coming up out of **139,685,000 square miles** of water. The earth is waiting for you to study it. The earth is saying to you, **"When I move you move, just like that."** Why shouldn't you travel and see it all? Why shouldn't you meet new people? Why shouldn't you become a trailblazer and go where no one in the history of your family has ever gone? You can choose to have a better attitude about the beautiful and magnificent world in which you live. You can choose to have a better attitude about your health within your own body. What's wrong with knowing more? Why should you remain ignorant about these things? How are you manifesting gratitude and appreciation to your Creator and to your parents if you don't become the best possible human being that you can be? You can do anything now that you know that your attitude about yourself is a little thing that makes a big difference!

Thank you for taking the time to read our first book, **"The Wise Men and Women Have Sent Me to Tell You".** To share your comments on this book please email us at marcusgirard34@yahoo.com. Our telephone number is **404-542-3808.** Please visit our website at www.marcusgirard.com for additional CD's and DVD's, products and services we offer and general information about Marcus Girard and the Youth and Adult Intervention Services.

Introducing the On-Line Counseling Center

When your child isn't acting right, just call Marcus Girard at 770-968-5801 to set up your telephone conference or On-line Conference! Visit us Online at: www.marcusgirard.com Or email us at: marcusgirard34@yahoo.com

"We specialize in giving young people a good old fashioned talking to!"

Keep up with the world of Brother Marcus at these sites:

Brother Marcus
Youth and Adult Motivational
Author, Speaker and Trainer:

Cell Phone - 404-542-3808
Website: www.marcusgirard.com
Email Address: marcusgirard34@yahoo.com
Hit Internet Radio Shows:
http://www.blogtalkradio.com/brothermarcusshow
My Health Products: www.immunotec.com/respect4life
Marcus Girard Pod Cast:
http://thebrothermarcusshow.mypodcast.com/index.html
Thank you and may God bless and keep you and your family!

Notes

Notes

Notes